Jesus Is Worth it all

Luke
Is 41:10

# DON'T TELL ANYONE YOU'RE READING THIS

# DON'T TELL ANYONE YOU'RE READING THIS

## A CHRISTIAN DOCTOR'S THOUGHTS ON SEX, SHAME, AND OTHER TROUBLESOME ISSUES

## LINA ABUJAMRA, MD

Forefront
BOOKS

*Don't Tell Anyone You're Reading This:*
*A Christian Doctor's Thoughts on Sex, Shame, and Other Troublesome Issues*

Copyright © 2023 by Lina AbuJamra

Scripture quotations are from The ESV® Bible (The Holy Bible, English
Standard Version®), copyright © 2001 by Crossway, a publishing ministry
of Good News Publishers. Used by permission. All rights reserved.

Published by Forefront Books.
Distributed by Simon & Schuster.
Published in association with Don Pape, Pape Commons.
www.papecommons.com

Library of Congress Control Number: 2023910824

Print ISBN: 978-1- 63763-218-5
E-book ISBN: 978-1-63763-219-2

Cover Design by Bruce Gore, Gore Studio, Inc.
Interior Design by Bill Kersey, KerseyGraphics

# DEDICATION

*To my nieces and nephews.*

*I'm hoping they're brave enough to read it.*

# CONTENTS

# DON'T SKIP THIS

*Birds do it, bees do it.*
*Even educated fleas do it.*
—Ella Fitzgerald

THERE ARE AT LEAST THREE WAYS CHRISTIANS THINK
about sex these days.

There's the prudish perspective. You're the
folks who were discipled in the eighties. You have
black-and-white notions about sex. You would *never*
be caught watching that movie or TV show that
everyone is talking about. You would *never* allow
yourself to read that trashy book and would *never*
click on that website. Most of you are married and
have occasional sex, and when you do, it's not that
exciting. You're used to blaming your spouse for your
bedroom stats. Most of you are white, saved by the
blood, and transformed forever. You have a Bible
verse for every problem in life that you're quick to
hand out to anyone you think is bleeding. You're
never going to admit to reading this book but might
make an extra effort to give it a one-star review on
Amazon. Just in case anyone else is tempted to read
it. Nice to meet you.

Then there's the millennial and younger perspective. You're much more avant-garde and hipster in
your approach to sex. You're not quite a hedonist,
because you're Christian after all, but God forbid
you be described as prudish! You started elementary

school around the time Steve Jobs dropped the first iPhone into the world. You grew up in a culture where sex and nudity have become the norm. Your access to X-rated content is one click away, and you're rolling your eyes at me right now. I mean, who needs yet another Christian book about sex, especially one written by a Christian author who is a fifty-year-old virgin at that—gulp. You are certain I'm about to embarrass myself and regurgitate a list of archaic do's and don'ts into the world. You're not even convinced that the list I'll share is in the Bible anyway. Swipe left. Move on.

But before you do, let me be clear about one thing. I'm also the doctor you'll be calling when you need your Plan B and birth control pills refilled, and when you're freaking out about that rash on your penis. It's okay. I'm not one to hold on to grudges. Plus, there are a couple of things you and I have in common: we share an extreme comfort talking about sex and a deep sense of compassion for sexual minorities. And we've both seen it all. So sit tight. You might actually like what I have to say (wink emoji).

And then there's the rest of us. We are not a category. We are not a specific age group or a demographic. We are normal Christians who never in a million years thought we'd still be wrestling with our sex lives. We are men *and* women who have experienced the awesome love of Jesus and received Him into our hearts with abandon. We committed to following Him. We read our Bibles and pray. We go to church and have Christian friends. We want to do right. We long to be more holy. Yet here we are, five, ten, or fifteen years into our Christian walk, and for the life of us, we can't figure out why we keep failing in this one area of our lives. We utterly hate that we still do what we hate. We know right from wrong and want to do right, but instead we are tired, broken, and maybe even cynical about change after all these years.

Oh, we have our good days, but our bad days are still far too common and repetitive, and our worst nightmare is that we be found out. We hate hypocrisy, yet we are living two lives. We hang on to the truth that God does remove our sins as far as the east is from the west, but lately, we're not even sure about that anymore. We feel we've overplayed our hand. We're not sure that change—at least for us—is possible.

We are weary from the battle inside us and we long to be free.

We are the church.

I don't know about you, but I'm sick of failing in my private life. I'm sick of worrying that if I don't get this right, my story will become a public debacle. I don't want a public reckoning of my sin. I just really want to change. I want to experience victory in my private life.

I decided to write this book one morning in January as I was scrolling through Instagram and landed on the news that yet another relatively famous Christian leader had been fired for moral failure.

The details were uncannily similar.

The only difference was that this time, I actually knew this worship leader! I had sat under his worship leading while attending a megachurch and serving on their staff. I had been deeply moved by his songs. I had watched him become the heart of our church's worship band. Most people who had been at the church for a decade or more were very well aware that this man had had a lapse in his moral journey when he was young and single. He was asked to leave his job as new worship leader back then, and two years later, he was repentant, forgiven, and reinstated. He then happily married and lived ever after. Or so it seemed. But all was not well in his private life.

For several months, this worship leader had led a secret affair. The rest, as they say, became tragedy.

How could this worship leader go from writing the most tenderhearted, touching worship songs about God on Sundays to hooking up with his mistress on Mondays? If this worship leader, whom I knew and respected, managed to make a mess of his life, what was keeping me from doing the same?

Something snapped in my brain when I read his story. The problem of sexual sin, a problem I am enlightened enough to know is rampant in the church, suddenly became very, very personal and very, very real.

Do you think I'm naive? Do I sound like an old-fashioned Christian who blushes at the word *sex* and still watches *Little House on the Prairie*? Think again. As a pediatric emergency physician, I've heard it all and I never blush. You can't shock me even if you tried. I've heard the good, the bad, and the ugly when it comes to sex. I am fully aware that humans have a sex drive and are motivated by lust. And I am fully aware that Christians struggle equally with lust and are taught to control that lust—often unsuccessfully.

I was in my late teens when I heard the salacious details of the fallen pastor at our tiny little Baptist church in Wisconsin. One day we showed up to Sunday night church and to the announcement that this leader had been removed from his role as pastor due to an extramarital affair. *Eww*, I thought to myself, *who would ever want to have sex with him?* Yet we sat on our pews, shaking our heads in bafflement. How could a pastor fall so quickly?

Since then, Christian leaders and their sexual failures have become the norm. Just about every week brings new gossip of another leader with a bombshell story. Like gnats at a barbecue, the rate of failure in Christian leadership has become so rampant it's hard to keep up. Lives have been ruined, families have been destroyed, and the church is imploding all for a few seconds of pleasure.

Few things have rocked the evangelical world in the last decade more than the news of Ravi Zacharias's sexual perversion. Here was the image of Christian virtue, a man whose very essence was the picture of integrity. He had been one of "us"—the untouchables. Yet today, Ravi's life and ministry have blown up into a million little pieces, leaving his victims wounded and some bleeding to death, others a pulp of their former life. How did a man like Ravi Zacharias spend his life teaching Christians to think, only to unravel posthumously, where it was evident that in his private world, he did anything but think?[1]

Over the years we've convinced ourselves that there are those who struggle with lust, like you and me, and then there are the pervs. They're the ones wasting their lives attending Celebrate Recovery meetings every week at church. They are typically men, and they indeed have a serious problem. They are porn addicts and sexual predators, and if we're being honest, we perhaps question their salvation. They are the reason their lives are unraveling. They barely even deserve our mercy.

Over the years we've divided the church into "us" and "them." We hear the statistics and nod our heads in agreement. Indeed, there is a problem in American Christianity. We assume the problem is out there and that we are somehow immune to it.

Stories like Ravi's shake us to the core because if a spiritual giant or a seemingly faithful worship leader has the capacity to fall so horrifically low, what's to say we won't?

The truth is that we're not immune to sexual struggle. We're not immune to failure. We're not immune to our lives unraveling at the speed of light because our wants and desires have taken over our thinking.

We need to understand why.

We need to understand why we continue to do the things we hate.

We need to understand why we can on one hand so easily talk about how sexualized our culture is and how bad the entertainment industry has become, while on the other hand secretly revel in the same smutty content that our nonbelieving friends openly admit to watching.

This book is not a book about porn. It's not a book about sexual purity and the rewards God gives to His sexually faithful followers. This is not a book about singles and sex, nor is it a book about married sex. God knows I don't know a thing about that.

This is a book about the struggle with our desires and why so many committed followers of Jesus are still failing in our sexual lives and how to change.

In other words, this is a book about sex for every Christian who longs to be free from sexual struggle.

It turns out that we all do it. We all struggle with some unwanted sexual desire or another. We all regularly give in to our sexual urges instead of choosing holiness. We all hold on to our favorite vices like little blankies, refusing to let go of them no matter what it costs. We fool ourselves into thinking that we're okay because no one has found out about our dirty little secrets yet, or because we've been clean for a month or a year. But we know that given enough time, we're going back there, to the comfort of our little blankies.

Instead, you and I are going to sit down and have a long talk about sex.

We're not going to talk about sex in the hush-hush way our parents did. We're not going to talk about sex in the voyeuristic and self-righteous way of judging others while enjoying the details of their dirty stories. We're not going to talk about sex in the shaming and judgmental way of reducing each person to our most basic sinful sexual instincts.

No.

Let's talk about sex in a very practical and real way that will finally lead us to freedom.

I'm sick of failing in my private life. I'm sick of worrying about whether someday there will be a public reckoning if I don't stop my own cycle of sin and shame.

Perhaps this is my public reckoning. I'm not willing to hide the truth anymore: I have struggled in my sex life, and I am tired of failing.

If you long for change and revival, and you dream of a day where the sun can finally break through into the darkness that has become your home, keep on reading.

If you're sick of watching Christian leaders fall with their harrowing stories of indiscretions and want to understand why the stories keep on happening, then keep reading.

If you're a Christ-following man or woman with a human body, keep reading.

It's time we have a real talk about sex.

# DENIAL

*I did not have sexual relations with*
*that woman, Ms. Lewinsky.*
—BILL CLINTON, 1998

I DON'T REALLY HAVE A PROBLEM WITH SEX. I MEAN, I've never even had sex. The first real date I had was to a citywide Bible study. I was in my mid-twenties. Yes, ma'am, I'm one of those weirdos. As a Lebanese-born follower of Jesus who moved to the USA at the end of my high school years, I still didn't know what a purity ring was, but I might as well have worn a shirt that said, "I'm a virgin and will stay that way until I'm married." Six months later, that man and I were engaged. Then two weeks before the wedding, we broke up.

I also got engaged to the second guy I dated seriously. This time, I was older and wiser, in my mid-thirties now. My plan was to enjoy kissing him until we got married. He pulled a fast one on me, though. He'd heard I was committed to staying pure until marriage. He told me he had decided to try something new. I suppose in hindsight, our paths had crossed at a time he was trying to stay clean. He told me he wanted to wait until the wedding day to kiss me. I wish I could say I had stars in my eyes, but I think what I saw that night in the mirror was just a transient bout of nausea. Needless to say, that relationship didn't last either.

I'm one of the few humans on this planet who can say that I was engaged to a man I never even kissed. So, you see why for years I told myself that I didn't have a problem with sex.

I worked with a Christian nurse once who showed up late to work. When we asked her why, she told us that her husband had been arrested by the FBI. We wanted to know why. I don't remember if her tears were angry or sad, but what she told us shocked us. This father of two, self-proclaimed Christian, was arrested for child porn. He had been monitored for some time by the FBI, and after the sting operation was completed, his house was raided and he was put in prison.

Now *this* was a guy who had a problem with sex.

I also knew a woman at my church who was married to a man addicted to porn. She found out about it one day, or maybe it was her child who found the porn. Needless to say, it put a dent in their love life. For years, he promised he'd get clean. He went to counseling. He went to rehab. He promised he'd never do it again. But he never could stop watching. A couple of decades later, she divorced him.

I guess you can say that *this* guy had a problem with sex too.

But not me. I don't have a problem with sex. Or as Eliza Doolittle liked to say, "I'm a good girl, I am!" I grew up in a Christian home. I went to a Christian and very strict university. I worked at a Christian camp every summer from my senior year in high school until I went to medical school. I didn't even have time for sex. And yet I have spent my entire adulthood trying to convince myself that I don't have a problem with sex. But why would I spend so much energy on something that wasn't a problem?

It took me two years of therapy to finally find the courage to talk about my sex baggage. I didn't know where to start. I was partly mad at God for holding out on me in what everyone else in the world seemed to enjoy. I was partly embarrassed by my own inability to get this one area of my life resolved. After stumbling through my story, I paused for a moment, then I made this statement:

"For someone who doesn't have a sex life, I sure spend a lot of time thinking about sex."

"You do have a sex life," my therapist responded. "You just don't have a healthy and fulfilling one."

I'd never thought about it that way.

Christians are funny about sex. We're a lot like the medical workers I know who spend their lives educating their patients about the harm of smoking, then huddle around the exit doors of the Emergency Department taking one last drag of their cigarettes. They call it an addiction, and it often is. While I appreciate the language of addiction when it comes to substance abuse, it's fascinating to see it cross over to the sexual struggles that are common in the Christian walk. Is it easier to use addiction language than to own up to our recurrent sexual mishaps? Does it feel more clinical and excusable to hide behind the label of addiction?

God, on the other hand, calls sinful sexual acts we can't stop doing slavery. It's a pretty harsh word but a lot more fitting. We are controlled by the things we obey. And for most of my life, I have had one master, represented by the letter *L*, for Lust.

Remember your high school mandatory reading list? The old *Scarlet Letter* still makes that list. Poor Hester Prynne. She knows what she's done, and to her credit, she owns it. She stands up straight on the scaffolding admitting her wrong. The people in the village can barely look at her. They are angered by her quiet dignity and honest beauty. For the rest of her life, she wears her scarlet letter, not with pride, but in truth. She is what she is, and she owns it. But not the father of her baby. He hides beneath the safety of his frock. He doesn't have the courage to admit that he's just like Hester—a slave to his own passions. But deep down, he knows. And he can't live with the guilt. Given enough time, he imposes his own punishment on himself. Eventually, everyone else in the village finds out too. By then, it's too late. Arthur Dimmesdale has already died.

Why are Christians in such deep denial over our sexual struggle? Why can't we stop pointing fingers at others and own that we are just as broken and desperate as everyone else? Even more perplexing, why can't we stop doing what we hate?

I hate statistics, but they do make a point.

- About half of Americans ages eighteen to thirty who are practicing Christians actively seek out porn at some point in a given year.
- One-fifth of practicing Christians ages eighteen to twenty-four actively seek out porn weekly.
- Over one in three practicing Christian millennials ages twenty-five to thirty actively seek out porn at least monthly.
- Nearly one in five practicing Christian married men actively seek out porn at least monthly.
- Fifteen percent of Christian women say they watch porn at least once a month.
- Only 13 percent of Christian women say they never watch porn.
- Over one in five youth pastors currently "struggle" with porn use.
- Over 94 percent of youth pastors and 92 percent of senior pastors believe porn is a bigger problem for the church now than it was twenty years ago.

- Protestants who believe that the Bible is the
  actual word of God and is to be taken literally
  are statistically identical to other Americans
  in most social media use.[2]

These are just porn stats! I haven't even started
listing the divorce statistics in the church, nor the
premarital fornication stats, nor the sexual abuse
stats in the church.

Yet today's Christians are standing on the rooftops waging a war against the culture over immorality. Christians are heartbroken over America's
drifting from a biblical sexual ethic. They have
sounded the alarm and are warning the culture to
beware of the fire that's coming while their own
homes are burning down and they linger inside,
unaware of the ashes rising up in their midst.[3]

Christians have somehow bought the rhetoric
that the greatest threat to American Christianity
is a liberal president, or a left-heavy House of
Representatives, or the gay agenda. Josh McDowell,
author and Christian leader, sees it differently and
he may be right. He says that it's porn that is the
greatest threat to American Christianity.[4]

The moment we neglected our own personal holiness is the moment we lost our voice in this culture.
There is a cognitive dissonance in the church. We all
know it. The millennials were the loudest to point

it out. They started leaving their churches in droves. Can you blame them?

The amount of energy Christ-following Christians have spent condemning sexual sin is exhausting. If only that same energy were spent on our own personal holiness.

I had a seventeen-year-old patient who came to the ER because she told her mom that she had a rash. When I finally made it to her room and asked her to show me her rash, she lifted her arm, and I saw a hole so big in her armpit I could almost put my entire fist in it. I looked at her mom with a horrified expression and asked why she hadn't brought her in sooner. The poor mom told me that she hadn't known about it until that day.

I looked at the patient whose eyes were downcast in shame. She was too embarrassed to answer my question. She was hunched over, desperate to hide. Shame doesn't always make a lot of sense. Was she ashamed for something she didn't even cause? Or was it shame because she had hidden for so long when she could have gotten better if only she'd come out of hiding and asked for help?

I waited a beat until she finally looked up with tears in her eyes, and that's when I recognized that face.

It was the face of denial.

You see, I'd worn that face before.

But not anymore.

My name is Lina, and I've never had sex, but I do have a problem with sex.

# CONTROL

*I'm so excited, and I just can't hide it.*
*I'm about to lose control and I think I like it.*
—THE POINTER SISTERS

THIS MIGHT BE A GOOD PLACE FOR ME TO PAUSE AND give you some definitions. What exactly do I mean when I use the word *sex*? *Lust*? *Sin*? Or even *porn*? Words can be confusing to say the least, so let me tell you what I mean when I use those surprisingly controversial words.

God created penises and vaginas. Even after four years in medical school and twenty-five years of medical practice, I find Genesis 2 still the best place to learn basic anatomy. While there are no schematics in Genesis, the image is clear. First God created man and named him Adam. Then God created Eve. God created them both male and female, Adam and Eve.[5] Penises and vaginas.

Adam knew his wife, Eve, and they had Cain. Or … Adam had sex with Eve, and they had a baby.

When God first talks about sex in the Bible, He refers to the intimate experience between a male and a female bound together through marriage. Marriage was God's idea from the start. The next step was for the newlyweds to go home and have sex and a lot of children.

We've come a long way since then, baby.

Most of us use the term *sex* much more loosely
these days. We use the term to refer to a wide variety
of activities meant to lead to arousal and orgasm.
Today, whether you agree with these practices or not,
sex can be between a man and a woman outside of
the context of marriage—the Bible calls that fornication if you're single and adultery if you're married.
Sex can be an act between two men or two women—
the Bible calls that homosexuality. Or it can mean
sex between two members of the same family—the
Bible calls that incest. Or it can mean sex between
a human and an animal—that's bestiality. Or it can
mean forcing sex on someone—the Bible calls that
rape. Or it can mean multiple people having sex
together—biblically speaking, that's an orgy. Or
there's sex that can be paid for—that's prostitution.
Or sex can mean stimulating oneself to orgasm—oh
yeah, that's masturbation. The *M* word is never used
in the Bible, but we created a word for it anyway
because we're, well, sexually savvy that way.

If you lump all those sex acts together, except
for sex between a husband and wife, you have what
God calls sexual sin or sexual immorality. Whenever
I use the words *sexual struggle* or *sexual immorality* in
this book, I'm adopting His view too. If you're not a
Bible-believing Christian, this is where you might be
tempted to stop reading the book and ask for your

money back. I can understand your frustration. I should have warned you from the start that this book is written with a biblical perspective for followers of Jesus, although I did think that my mentioning the fact that I am a fifty-year-old virgin would have given that up. But hold up a second. Maybe it's wishful thinking on my part, but I'd love for you to stick around a little bit longer. I have a feeling that we have a lot more in common than you think.

Anyway, what about lust? What exactly is lust? The dictionary defines lust as an intense and unrestrained sexual craving or an overwhelming desire or craving.[6] The Bible always uses the term *lust* with a negative connotation to reflect sinful longing. I like to think of lust as wanting something at the wrong time and in the wrong amount. Furthermore, lust doesn't always relate just to sex. You can lust after stuff, too, like cars and houses. I have spent hours scrolling through Instagram lusting after other people's kitchens and gardens. The tricky part about lust is that it's not an action. It's more like an idea, a thought. But it's even more nuanced. Because even if you're one of those Christians who says they follow Jesus but doesn't particularly like the Bible, you've got to figure out what to do with what Jesus said about lust in Matthew 5:27–28: "You have heard that it was said, 'You shall not commit adultery.' But I say to you that everyone who looks at a woman with lustful intent has already committed adultery with her in his heart."

I guess none of us is that innocent after all now, are we?

Then there's porn. What exactly is porn? Well, to start with, it's bad. The word *porn* comes from the Greek word *porneia*, used twenty-six times in the New Testament. The word *porneia* is a generic term for sexual sin, including sexual immorality, fornication, marital unfaithfulness, prostitution, and adultery. That's a whole lot of troublesome stuff packed into one word.[7] *Porn* is short for *pornography* and is the depiction of erotic behavior intended to cause sexual excitement. It is usually conveyed through materials such as books, photos, or videos in a way that arouses humans quickly.[8] Supreme Court justice Potter Seward summed it up well in 1964. He said about pornography, "I know it when I see it." According to Barna, most of us not only know it when we see it but have also seen it at one point or another too.[9]

Are you still tracking? I can summarize it all like this: according to God's Word, the Bible, the only sexual relationship God blesses is between one man and one woman in the context of marriage. Everything else is sexual sin. Pornography is just one form of sexual sin that is really, really bad.

What's ironic is that most Bible-believing Christ followers say they hold to this orthodox biblical worldview and completely agree with my definitions so far yet are still, according to statistics, living a lie. We have a puzzling paradox: we morally reject sexual immorality but still regularly participate in sexual sin in one form or another. Maybe not all the time, but enough to wonder. Why do we do what we don't want to do? And why do we want to so badly? If we didn't want to so much, maybe we would stop.

I haven't done a poll yet, but in the scientific way of most ER doctors (i.e., my gut instinct), I would venture to guess that there isn't a Christian leader whose life has imploded by sex scandal who didn't at one point tell themselves, "I can stop this anytime." I've told myself the very same thing in a million different ways. I can stop anytime. I've got this. There's nothing to worry about here. I don't have a problem. I can control how far this goes. Guess how successful I've been at doing that? Yeah, right.

I practice my porn through reading. Too soon to fess up? Well, the cat's out of the bag now. I suppose you can say that I'm a "respectable" sinner. None of that computer screen nonsense—for the most part. My pattern of sin is typical for women. Don't believe me? Consider two words: Colleen Hoover. I just checked the Amazon bestseller list and can confirm that there are not one, two, or even three Colleen

Hoover all-around-best-selling books, but FIVE in the top twenty-five.[10] That's a lot of people reading a lot of steamy romance novels. Hoover admits she writes at least one erotic sex scene in each of her books.[11]

I started off reading pretty vanilla love stories. It was a good way to kill time. I used to scour the *Reader's Digest* G-rated love stories back in the eighties. It didn't take me long to move to steamier novels. I didn't think I had a problem back then. It was just innocent reading. I mean, who didn't love a kid who checks out books at the library? I had things under control. I'd grow out of the habit soon, especially when life got busier in college. While school did eventually occupy my time, summers off were the perfect time to unwind and pick up old habits. For someone who studied all the time, finding an escape in fiction was a gift I cherished.

I noticed that I started pushing the envelope on sexual reading content with time. What used to satisfy me didn't anymore. I remained under the illusion that I was master of my impulses. In time, I got used to juggling my sin habit with my Christian responsibilities quite successfully, I might add. I was still convinced I could kick the habit anytime I wanted to. It was just a matter of deciding when I needed to. My plan was always that I'd get married and start living a real love life instead of a fictional one. I think we can agree by now that that was wishful thinking. Three decades later, not only were things spiraling out of control but I was wading in waters with riptides threatening to pull me under.

I wish I could do what others have done and shake off what I know to be true. I would tell myself to stop denying myself. Be free. Express myself. Run like a cheetah in the wild and be who I was meant to be. But where does it stop? When are one's impulses finally expected to be controlled? Is there ever a line in the sand where we must indeed finally deny ourselves? And says who? What if what looks like self-denial to you is different than what it means to me? Who gets to decide where the line in the sand is drawn?

Is it finally bad when one moves from a book to a screen? And how much porn on a screen is bad? Does a minute matter, or is it bad only if you spend more than five minutes on a website? Are images as bad as videos? Are sexual images between a man and a woman more acceptable than images between two men or two women? What about age groups? Is it more acceptable the day after someone's eighteenth birthday? And is porn bad when it's on a porn site but more acceptable if it's built into the storyline of a movie? Where do you draw the line? When does control overrule the great spirit of sexual freedom we've been told we deserve?

We talk about control, but what control? The moment you allow lust a toehold into your mind is like letting a mouse into your house. Before you know it, an entire population of mice is squatting in your attic. It's impossible to get rid of them without a miracle.

We naively think we're the exception to the rule. We figure that even though everyone else has absolutely no control over their lust, somehow we do. If it were that easy to just say no to sexual sin, most pastors who have blown up their lives and ministries due to a sex scandal would have stopped before their demise. If it were that easy to just say no, I would have done it back in my *Reader's Digest* days. If it were that easy to simply turn off our sexual impulses and just say no to sexual sin, we wouldn't be hearing about 68 percent of churchgoing men and 50 percent of pastors who regularly view porn. Or the 76 percent of Christians age eighteen to twenty-four who actively and regularly spend time searching porn sites. Or the only 13 percent of self-identified Christian women who say they never watch porn (which leaves 87 percent of Christian women who have at some point watched porn).[12]

What usually starts out as a small and innocent sin can quickly morph into a cascade of more shocking sins than we ever dreamed we would commit.

How easily we lose control.

Ironically, in every other area of our lives, we tend to be control freaks.

I've seen over 150,000 patients in the last seven years as a telehealth provider. I know because we keep track of every measurable detail in telehealth. And here's what I've learned from my vast experience with people: humans are indeed control freaks. We try to control almost every single situation in life. Some of us try to control outcomes by using anger and threats. For example, my patients will warn me that if I don't give them what they want, they'll report me to someone. Others of us use kindness to control the outcomes in our lives. We think if we smile enough and say thank you enough, the person on the other side of the counter will do what we want. Still, others of us use emotions like humor or tears to control situations.

No matter the strategy we use, when all is said and done, most of us are control freaks except when it comes to the things that we ought to control—like our anger, or our spending, or our eating, or, as I've come to learn, my lust. When it comes to stopping certain sinful sexual patterns in my life, I get a big fat F. Why is that? Why can't I stop doing what I know as a follower of Jesus that I shouldn't be doing?

I've been told that I have an addictive personality. Is that why it seems impossible to control my sexual impulses? While my sexual impulses don't seem to have harmed anyone else in life so far but me, try telling that to the victim of rape or abuse, or even to the wife of the pastor who has just been told that her husband has been having a six-month-long affair with someone else. I don't buy it. I can't give in to the notion of pinning sexual mishaps on addiction. It just feels lazy and dishonest.

Why then are so many of us unable to control what we so naively thought we could? Whether it's the porn addict who promises his wife that he can stop anytime, or the woman who swears she'll never have another one-night stand, or the Christian couple planning to marry but still single and vowing never to go that far again, we seem powerless in the areas of our lives where we need to be! It's exhausting to say the least.

Here's a thought: what if we fail in controlling our sexual sin not because we can't control it but because we like it? What if the reason we keep going back to the place that we hate and do the things we abhor is that deep down, doing what we hate makes us feel better about what our deeper problem is? Perhaps our sexual sin is really the lesser of two evils.

That's something worth stopping and thinking about.

There's one more thing to consider when it comes to why we have a hard time controlling our own sexual sin and our lust. What if we're just going about it all wrong? Have you ever wondered why people like Joseph, the guy with the amazing technicolor dream coat, did have the ability to control his lust and run from the vixen wife of Potiphar, while David, God's chosen man, succumbed to his lust like a feeble old woman? What did Joseph have that David didn't? And why is it still so much easier to connect with David on this?

Have you ever bought anything at Ikea? God help us, so have I. The story is always the same. We go to the store and walk around until we spot the piece of furniture we want. We make our way to the stock room and finally overcome the challenge of putting the box in the back of our car. You know exactly what's coming. After opening the box and setting out all the pieces on the floor, we start building that wretched table. We muddle our way through the first few steps hoping we don't lose our religion in the process. And then it happens. The problem of the missing piece. No matter how hard we try to put that piece of furniture together and make it work, there is *always* a missing piece.

Trying to control my own sexual impulses has long felt like an Ikea project. No matter how hard I try to control my own lust, it's like there's always a missing piece. Lately I've been thinking, *What if that's our problem? What if all of us Christians still struggling with lust are trying to control our problem while missing the missing piece?* My whole life I've acted as if the missing piece has been my ability to say no to sin strongly and decisively enough. My whole life I've assumed that the missing piece is my own willpower over my flesh. But what if that's not the missing piece at all?

What if the missing piece is Jesus? Remember when we were in junior high and we felt like it was our duty to shelter our parents from R-rated movies? The minute they walked into the room and caught us watching something racy, we quickly changed the channel. We didn't think they could handle that stuff, or maybe it was our own guilt in action. I catch myself doing the same thing with Jesus. Maybe it's time to invite Him into the stadium to help me fight my battles instead of acting like He doesn't even know what sex is or is as uncomfortable with it as I am.

What if Jesus is the missing piece in our struggle for control? Instead of trying so hard to say no to our sin, what if instead we focused on saying yes to Jesus?

# EXCUSES

*Ooh, look what you made me do.*
*Look what you made me do.*
—TAYLOR SWIFT

I WATCHED A SHOW ABOUT A BANK HEIST ONCE. IT made me think of the church. In one scene, the people who had been at the bank that day were all put in one room while the masked robbers terrorized them half to death. Throughout the show, the robbers would simply walk around the room with guns in their hands, sometimes taunting the innocents, sometimes doing nothing but pacing up and down the rows, their very presence a threat. Little by little, the robbers started picking the prisoners out one by one and taking them to another room for a showdown and certain death. Occasionally, some of the prisoners became so tired of resisting that they changed sides. They joined the ranks of the terrorists.

The picture of the prisoners being terrorized by the robbers is not unlike what's happening in the American church today. Christians are held at gunpoint by sexual temptation and are falling one by one, starting with the leaders. When asked why this is happening, we are quick to blame the evil one, Satan.

Remember the Church Lady on *SNL* back in the eighties? "Well, isn't that special? Now who could it be? Could it be . . . Satan?"[13] Dana Carvey played the

Church Lady in a sketch that became quite popular mocking Christians' tendency to blame Satan for everything. Not much has changed since then. We Christians do tend to blame Satan for most of our mishaps, especially when it comes to sexual sin and immorality.

I've done it before. While at times my blaming Satan is on point, I wonder if all too often, I'm just coming up with excuses.

One of the most common scapegoats for sexual sin is that we're living in an ultra-hypersexual culture. Sex, sex, sex. Everywhere we look, it's sex all the time everywhere. There's sex on TV and sex on the billboards. Sex in the news and sex in our homes. Gone are the Puritan days of America. We're now living in a world where sex sells, and it sells a whole lot. Therefore, sex is everywhere. Before 2007 (the year the iPhone was first dropped), the simplest way to access porn was through sex stores, and only creepers went there. Today, Satan has moved the action into our homes, taunting Christ followers with the truth that we're not as strong as we think we are. Given the gift of anonymity, we're not that much holier than everyone around us. We're just as broken inside.

About a decade ago, I was fighting hard to do the right thing. I had reinstalled the parental restrictions on my phone and deleted any app that led me down the path to darkness. There was one loophole I couldn't control. No matter how hard I tried, Amazon still wouldn't allow me to restrict access to sexual content. I emailed Amazon. I imagined someone in the Philippines trying to understand what I was asking. Maybe that's why I never got an answer. It's been easy for me to keep blaming Amazon for my struggle.

Excuses, excuses.

Here's another one that's overly used. Can we talk about the clothes we're not wearing these days? Men claim that it's not their fault they can't control themselves. They say it's the women who are practically naked that are to blame. I've watched the modesty debate unfold over and over on social media. Conservative Christians ridiculed for trying to win the culture war by advocating for more modesty in the culture. Other Christians fighting for their rights to wear whatever they want to wear. I'm not trying to be your grandma here, but sometimes I think we've lost our senses on the modesty debate. Daisy Dukes litter the church auditorium on a Saturday evening service. Christian Instagram pics flood our feeds with Bachelorette-looking women with a peculiar mix of #Jesus and #checkoutmybodyinthisthong.

It's not just the ladies who have joined the culture in our right to wear whatever we want movement. The men are guilty too.

There's this iconic picture of former celebrity pastor Carl Lentz walking down the boardwalk practically naked next to Justin Bieber. Justin who? All my eyes could focus on was that V on Lentz's lower abs. A year later, Lentz's ministry blew up from sexual sin. Were his board shorts to blame? Did the devil make him do it? Who knows. Who cares. Either way, using hollow excuses to justify our own sinful behaviors doesn't work. Our list of excuses is endless and paper thin.

It's easier to blame others than to accept responsibility for who we are. We're not the first to do it. Adam taught us all about blame shifting way back in the garden. When caught with his hand in the apple jar, he blamed Eve for his sin. When Eve was called out, she blamed the snake. Who do you blame for your sin? Jesus's perspective was different—as His ways always are. He understood that while the heist led by the bank robbers ultimately reveals who we are, our main problem lies deep within us. Here are His exact words in Mark 7:15–23:

> "There is nothing outside a person that by going into him can defile him, but the things that come out of a person are what defile him." And when he had entered the house and left the people, his disciples asked him about the parable. And he said to them, "Then are you

also without understanding? Do you not see that whatever goes into a person from outside cannot defile him, since it enters not his heart but his stomach, and is expelled?" (Thus he declared all foods clean.) And he said, "What comes out of a person is what defiles him. For from within, out of the heart of man, come evil thoughts, sexual immorality, theft, murder, adultery, coveting, wickedness, deceit, sensuality, envy, slander, pride, foolishness. All these evil things come from within, and they defile a person."

We don't have a behavior problem; we have a heart problem.

While it's been easy for me to make a list of all my excuses for failing in my sex life, what has helped me a whole lot is to try to come up with some explanations.

What makes a worship pastor with a beautiful wife and beautiful kids and a record deal and everything to live for give it all up for an orgasm? What makes a famous pastor of a megachurch who led the biggest leadership conference in America crucify his reputation for the sake of his sexual urges? What makes one of the most prolific authors and thinkers in the Christian world take advantage of vulnerable women and almost get away with it? And what makes you and me continue to hang on to what we know is wrong even when we understand what it will cost us to be found out?

Did you know that most people get addicted to pain killers because of pain? Hardly anyone plans on a future of addiction to narcotics. Typically, patients go to their doctors because they're hurting. They're started on pain meds. If the pain is not dealt with effectively, it's only a matter of time before more pain meds are given, and eventually an addiction develops. It's the same way with our sexual sin. Or at least it was for me.

As a teenager with raging hormones, finding sexual release in the pages of an erotic novel might seem normal, but it didn't take long for me to develop a pattern where I found refuge and connection in the safety of a book. I was never a very popular kid in school. I wasn't the kind of girl that guys asked out. I was a nerd in high school. I moved from Beirut, Lebanon, to Green Bay, Wisconsin, as a senior in high school and graduated when I was only sixteen years old. Needless to say, no one asked me to prom that year. In college, I was too smart for my own good, and still a teenager. No one asked me out then either. You feeling sorry for me yet? My sad story only gets worse. I finally met a guy in my pediatric residency and started dating for the first time in my mid-twenties. Alas, the engagement ended two weeks before the wedding, which added to my angst. My then best friend whom I had hoped would marry me decided to marry someone else.

If this isn't a recipe for disaster, I don't know what is. I spent so many years so deep in self-pity that the only safe place I found any kind of comfort was in romance novels that always ended in happily ever after. The longer I was single, the worse my problem became. In my thirties, I assumed I'd eventually marry, so I took great care to manage my reading boundaries. After a second broken engagement, all bets were off. No matter how hard I looked, my best option for love was through fiction. I am not sure when my behavior crossed the line from normal to obsessive and addictive, but eventually it did. You can't still blame your sinful habits on your raging hormones once you hit your perimenopausal years, can you?

It sounds so pathetic, but I don't think I'm alone. One of the biggest surprises I've had to come to terms with in my Christian life is the fact that temptation does not get easier with time. Sometimes, it only gets harder.

Then there was the God factor.

Where was God in my pain? Why hadn't He done anything to bail me out of my own misery? I've always had very little faith in humanity. My cynicism was made worse year after year of practicing medicine in the ER. I've never expected much from people, but I've always expected a lot from God.

In my thirty-year-old mind's eye, I was the bank teller held up at gunpoint in a room filled with terrorists, refusing to give in to fear, knowing beyond a shadow of a doubt that freedom was around the corner. I refused to give in to despair, confident that at any moment in time, Jesus would set me free. Perhaps I thought freedom would come in the form of a husband, but at the very least, I assumed freedom would come in the form of control over my sexual urges. But freedom never came. My life became more challenging. My faith became more fractured. I eventually wrote a book about it that I fittingly called *Fractured Faith*. I moved from blaming the hypersexualized culture, then Jeff Bezos and Amazon, then my own failure at dating, to eventually blaming God.

Why does a God who could change our broken desires not do anything about them? Why does a God who could provide a solution to our pain not show up when we need Him the most? Some of us act out by sinning to show Him how angry and hurt and confused we are. Some of us turn to sin because we feel we deserve the shame. It's like a self-fulfilling prophecy. Some of us turn to sin because it's what we were taught in our early childhood. We settle for a few moments of pleasure even though we know it could be costing us our life.

Why have I chosen the momentary gratification of my sexual sin over the faith-filled walk of self-denial? Maybe deep down I just want to be loved and affirmed and wanted. The less we experience God's goodness in our lives in tangible ways, the more we're apt to look for love in the wrong places. In our moments of need, we turn to anyone and anything that is willing to give us a quick shot of love, as fragile and imaginary as it might be.

We make excuses for our bad decisions because it's easier than dealing with our actual problems.

Excuses allow us to justify what we're doing just a little bit longer.

Excuses allow us to enjoy what we're doing without feeling so much pain.

Excuses allow us the privilege of hiding.

Excuses delay the need to fix what's really broken inside us, because fixing the problem can be so exhausting.

Excuses are a way to avoid negative consequences that might come when enough courage is mustered to live truthfully.

We make excuses and stick to them because it's too painful and scary to admit the truth of who we are and to admit how perverted our desires are. Excuses pass the blame from us to other factors. If we can convince God that we didn't have a choice in the matter, perhaps He might afford us a little bit of mercy.

For most of my life, I have succumbed to the same temptation over and over again.

For most of my life, I have been broken and hungry for love.

For most of my life, I have been waiting for God to show up in the way that I want Him to.

For most of my life, I have been hurting. While I'm not offering any excuses, perhaps what I'm giving you is simply an explanation.

# SECRETS

*We're only as sick as the secrets we keep.*

—MARIA NEMETH

*And be sure your sin will find you out.*

—NUMBERS 32:23

I SAT IN MY THERAPIST'S OFFICE DEBATING WHETHER I should tell her my deepest secret. The longer I waited, the worse I felt about it, and the less I wanted to tell her. My secret festered like mold on cheese. What would she think of me once I told her the truth? Would she still want to be my therapist? What if I told her and nothing in my life changed? Or worse—what if I told her and everything in my life had to change?

I kind of liked the way things were.

I hung on to the status quo as long as I could. I told myself that no one would ever find out. I convinced myself that I could enjoy what I was doing just a little while longer. If it really was a big deal to God, He would have punished me by now.

The thing about secrets is that the longer you wait, the harder it is to confess them. They start taking on a life of their own.

I had a weird thing happen to me in my third year of medical school. I went in to see my first ever patient on my family medicine rotation. I had never examined a live patient before, and I was scared out of my mind. I got through the history and told the man to put on a gown so I could do his physical exam. I stepped out of the room while he changed.

I came back to do the exam and went through the entire sequence of the examination, including the rectal exam. When I finished, I stepped to the sink to wash my hands. I started to take off my gloves, and that's when I noticed that in my angst over getting everything right, I'd forgotten to put on gloves in the first place.

I couldn't breathe for a minute. What should I do? Do I tell anyone about it? What will they think? I was mortified. So I did absolutely nothing at all. Well, I did wash my hands. I then proceeded to finish the visit, staff it with the attending physician, and went home. I never told a soul. I simply put the incident in a box on a shelf way up where I couldn't reach it.

It took me ten years before I was ready to reach up and open that box again. By then, I was well into my career and had a much higher level of confidence in my ability as a physician. I was the attending physician now and already loved by the residents I was training, so I didn't worry about what they would think of me. We were swapping medical war stories, and the grittier the story, the more awe was shown. I had a gritty story all right. It was time to break out the box. It was a risk I had to take, but oh, I had a feeling it would be worth it. And it was. Unleashing my secret brought a new sense of freedom. I started telling the story from time to time at speaking engagements. For years now, the very secret that had paralyzed me has become a way for me to connect with other people.

We keep secrets because we're ashamed of what we've done. We keep secrets because we want others to think the best of us. Deep down we're all a little bit scared of what others will think of us. We create a facade, an image that we try to protect at all costs. If only we understood the freedom that comes from revealing those secrets.

I made a mental list of pastors and Christian leaders whose lives have imploded by sexual scandal in the last ten years. I didn't use Google. I didn't include the seven hundred names of pastors on the Southern Baptist list of sexual abusers.[14] I didn't bother with small-town nameless pastors. Some of the names are so well known you can recognize them by just one name, like Oprah or Beyoncé.

I came up with twenty-three names. All men. All with a secret life that no one knew about until they did. Are you appalled by this? Are you scratching your head wondering how these guys could be naive enough to think that no one would ever find out?

It turns out they're not alone in living secret lives.

Humans have three lives: public, private, and secret. Psychologists have proven that we all harbor secrets. A study in the *Journal of Personality and Social Psychology* identified thirty-eight common categories of secrets that people keep about themselves. They found that 97 percent of people have a secret in at least one of those categories, and the average person is currently keeping secrets in thirteen of those categories![15] If you're wondering what those categories are, you are correct to assume that most of them are about sex.

Keeping secrets seems to be the human way. We think no one will ever find out. We don't really know one another as well as we think we do. At any given time, you might be talking with someone who is hiding a secret addiction to drugs or alcohol. At any given time, you might be talking to someone who once had an abortion they are keeping secret. At any given time, you might be talking to someone who is cheating on their spouse, unhappy in their marriage, experiencing same-sex attraction, or financially unraveling. That's not counting the weird fetishes people have among other counternormative behaviors.

We all have secrets that we think no one will ever find out. But eventually people do find out. It's the way of life.

For people like Jeffrey Dahmer, it was the smell emanating from his kitchen that led to his arrest as a serial killer with a bend toward chopping people up and putting the pieces in his freezer.[16] You don't have to be as deranged as Dahmer to keep secrets, but for better or for worse, we all have our own well-kept secrets.

For pastors and Christian leaders, secrets are kept because there's too much at stake if the truth comes out. Take, for example, a man like Ravi Zacharias, who had written too many books and accepted too many speaking invitations to share his dirty little secret with the world. He not only had a reputation to uphold but a lifestyle to keep up as well. So, he learned to hide his secret in a box on a shelf, making sure it never interfered with his ministry work.

It's called compartmentalization.

We do that very well in the ER in an effort to cope. We divide our minds into separate sections and categories. We do it to survive. We shove all our unwanted mental baggage and perverted behavior into a closet and slam the door really tight.

It's how pastors are able to preach so convincingly on Sunday and abuse their parishioners so thoroughly on Monday. It's how men show up to their kids' soccer games and act like the devoted husband and father while leading a secret affair on the side. If we shut the door to the closet tightly enough, we figure no one will try and open it. For too many Christians, this strategy has worked for too long.

We equate God's silence with His approval. We misunderstand that God's temporary silence is more like His mercy—waiting for us to step into the light.

If we insist on hiding secrets that are hurting others, God finally steps in. Sometimes it doesn't feel like He steps in soon enough, but He does always step in with justice and mercy.

He did it in the garden when Adam and Eve chose to hide from Him. He stepped into King David's life after he committed his heinous sin. Think about it. David thought he had gotten away with his sin. He had abused his power and slept with Bathsheba, who was married to Uriah. She got pregnant. David then had her husband killed.[17] He was the king, after all. He could do anything. He thought he had managed the whole thing impeccably, except that God had witnessed it all. Why didn't God step in before Bathsheba's husband, Uriah, was killed? It doesn't seem fair. Maybe it's a reminder to us that our secrets always come with a price. Just ask King David what a wrecking ball his little secret had on his life. The cost for a night of pleasure was higher than he might have wanted to pay.

When I was in my twenties, I used to live in fear of the fact that God saw every little thing I did. One of my primary motivations to stop sinning back then was the idea that Jesus might come back while I was masturbating. I couldn't think of anything worse that could happen to me. Everyone else would be reading their Bibles while I hid under the sheets trying to get an orgasm. It scared me enough to stop for a while.

Even now, the idea that I may be found out has continued to drive me to clean things up. What if I died and someone found my iPhone? What would they think? How embarrassing would that be? So I make sure I clear the history in my phone and delete any questionable content—just in case.

Fear is a temporary motivator to do the right thing. Only love can change the heart. Love, it turns out, is a far better motivator for change. Well, love and a healthy dose of humility.

I finally did tell my therapist my deepest secret. One of my fears was that I would be rejected by her once the truth about who I was came out. Instead, I was met with compassion. I was given understanding. Love has made all the difference in the world to me.

I am aware that some secrets are worse than others. I understand that you might be struggling with a secret that could incur the wrath of humanity against you if and when it becomes known. That's a difficult place to live. You can already see the repercussions of coming clean. All we need to do is look at the Catholic Church or the Southern Baptists and see the effect that unveiling secrets has had to understand how bad things can be. But this kind of pain is necessary on the journey to wholeness. I also remind myself that even though I experienced compassion from my therapist when I came clean, it's not her love that I needed. It's God's love that I crave. It's God's love that heals us.

Someone recently asked me how I continue to experience the goodness of God in my life after some of the challenges that I've been through. Honestly? It's when I'm at my worst and need God the most that I sense His goodness the nearest.

I've often wondered what would have happened if Ravi Zacharias had admitted his wrong and forsaken his hurtful ways. Would the story of his life have ended differently? While he might have lost some of his fans, I think he would have gained his integrity. I wish he had come clean when he still could.

There are four outcomes for any person who is living a secret life:

Outcome #1: You get away with it for a little while.

Outcome #2: You get caught.

Outcome #3: You admit what you're doing and keep doing it because you've convinced yourself it's not wrong.

Outcome #4: You confess what you're doing and change. This is called repentance.

Far too many Christians in our day and age have chosen outcome #3. Instead of fighting for a life of truth, they've chosen to redefine truth to suit their sinful impulses. Sexual sin is redefined based on cultural preference instead of on a biblical perspective. Divorce becomes the norm. Same-sex relationships become acceptable. And so on.

True confession is radically different. It stops prioritizing me. True confession sees the hypocrisy of living a lie and comes to a point where the pleasure of continuing the sinful behavior pales in comparison to the pain of continuing to live a double life. True confession stops caring about what people will think and starts to comprehend that what God thinks matters more. True confession becomes willing to let go of personal reputation and the security of a comfortable life for the sake of a clear conscience. In other words, true confession finally chooses God over me.

This is *my* true confession.

# BILLY GRAHAM RULE

*Women need a reason for having sex,*
*men just need a place.*
—Billy Crystal

*For the times they are a-changin'.*
—Bob Dylan

THERE IS SOMETHING SO FUNDAMENTALLY FUNDA-
mentalist about the Billy Graham rule and purity
culture. If you're over thirty, you don't need an explanation of these terms, but for all the millennials and
younger, let me try and explain.

Billy Graham, a man born in 1918 and respon-
sible for a movement of revival based out of
stadiums, gathered with his cronies one day and
set up a list of resolutions they called a manifesto
to help them keep their integrity as their movement
grew.[18] Billy became famous with time, and as can
happen, everyone wanted to copy everything he did—
including his set of rules.

Billy Graham died in 2018 at the ripe age of just
shy of one hundred. He never had an affair, which is
evidently a lot to say. Many point to his sacred rules
as the reason for his sexual success.

Christians have made a big fuss about the Billy
Graham rule, in particular, the resolve never to spend
any one-on-one time with a member of the opposite
sex unless it was his immediate family. Christians
have a love/hate relationship with the Billy Graham
rule. Some love it and still hold on to it. Others point
out its ridiculousness and are quick to criticize it.

Here's my take on the Billy Graham rule: it's not a bad rule, but it's outdated.

Think about it. Pragmatically speaking, no one ever committed adultery in the presence of three people; well, unless you're talking threesomes. I'm not being crass. I did in fact hear of a pastor and his wife who were fired from their church because they had a single female member of their church staff living with them, and well, let's just say the Billy Graham rule might not have made a difference for those three.

Our relational world today has moved away from lunch in the office to the vastness of the world wide web. The Billy Graham rule makes no stipulations for sexting, DMing, or online affairs. When I worked at the children's hospital in Chicago, I found it awkward to have lunch alone with my married colleagues. So I avoided it. The only guy I felt comfortable hanging one-on-one with was my gay colleague. These days I don't have an office. Just because I don't have to worry about whether or not I should have lunch with another man doesn't mean I have been excluded from sexual temptation. There's another aspect to the Billy Graham rule that I've experienced. As a result of the fear stirred up by the Billy Graham rule, pastors have become especially odd when it comes to interacting with women. It's probably worse because I'm a single woman, but I'm tired of feeling like a sexual vixen anytime I say hi to a pastor at a church.

I often wonder what Jesus might have made of the Billy Graham rule. He sure broke it on that day by the well with the sexually experienced woman from Samaria. He lived to tell the story.

The other interesting phenomenon in Christian sex education of a bygone era is the purity culture. This was a movement attempting to promote a biblical view of purity by discouraging dating and promoting virginity before marriage. The purity movement used tools like purity pledges and purity rings, and it hosted events like purity balls to get teens excited about the concept of life without sex until marriage. Again, not a horrible idea, but kinda outdated—plus, even Miley Cyrus has moved on.

I went to a college that was known for its pink and blue sidewalks. Well . . . not literally, but people still believe that rumor. We certainly had our own version of purity culture. We had a dating parlor and a three-foot rule for couples who went on a date. Am I embarrassed to admit these facts about my alma mater? No. Not at all. I find it quite amusing. What's baffling is that despite these stringent rules, many couples still managed to find a way to get pregnant. I never dated in college, which means that I never experienced the dating parlor, but I also never risked getting pregnant.

Then there's Joshua Harris. He was a big advocate of the purity culture. He was a good-looking celebrity pastor who wrote a dating manifesto while he was still single. I was mildly influenced by Harris's book *I Kissed Dating Goodbye*, mostly in the way that someone who never dated felt vindicated that perhaps I was doing something right. Joshua was all in on all things purity. He later married the love of his life, which elevated his status in the eyes of Christians everywhere. A couple of decades later, he repudiated his purity views, divorced his wife, and deconstructed his faith.[19]

The problem with rules, whether it's in the form of the Billy Graham rule or the purity culture, is that it sets us up for failure. It's about legalism, and legalism never wins. Legalism sets up the ridiculous expectation that if I do my part, God is obliged to do His. God isn't obliged to do anything, let alone provide you with a happy and sexually fulfilling marriage. Anything He gives us is pure grace.

Yet today, all across American churches are single men and women who have bought into the lie that if we remain pure before marriage, God will give us a happy marriage and a great sex life. And all across American churches today are couples who waited until marriage to have sex and still ended up with a disappointingly bad sex life.

Instead of focusing on purity rings and preacher rules, pastors have the God-given privilege to teach men two things: why keeping it in your pants until you get married shows your respect for women, and that when you finally do get married, sex isn't about you getting an orgasm. It's about you honoring the woman God has given you by giving her a reason to want to have sex with you. And that sex isn't about the act. It's about connection. It's about your heart.

It's time to move past basic anatomy, don't you think?

# NAVEL GAZING

*Idle hands are the devil's workshop.*
(PROVERBS 16:27)

*Boredom: the desire for desires.*
—LEO TOLSTOY

LATE AT NIGHT IS WHEN THE TRUTH DARES MAKE ITS way to the surface.

I am bored. How is it possible for me to be bored? But it's there, this gnawing feeling that something is missing.

No matter how hard I try to busy my life with activity, I'm restless. Dissatisfied. In the daytime, I squash these thoughts with more work. More activity. I beat the questions down like a ten-year-old playing Whac-A-Mole at the fair. But at night, the truth creeps out of the closet.

I am bored.

I have lived my life waiting for something big to happen. I waited for my big love and was crushed when it passed me by. I waited for my big break in the Christian ministry world. Instead, I was told I could stay for the show but was invited to make my way to the overflow room. I've waited for the Red Sea to part, the walls of Jericho to crumble, Lazarus to storm out of the tomb.

I'm still waiting.

Nighttime is when I feel it the most, this sense of emptiness. The feeling that this is it. This is my life in a nutshell. I'm alone and dissatisfied and sad. I will wake up tomorrow morning and have to do it all over again. The hustle, the sprint, the endless attempt to keep it all together just in case something big is around the corner.

But here in the middle of the night, I am free to admit that I am bored and alone.

All I've ever wanted was a big adventure with God.

I try opening my Bible and reading a few verses, but I feel nothing at all. I don't know what I'm looking for, what I'm straining to hear. It's easier to fill the void with something, anything. So I do the obvious. Systematically I make my way through the apps: Netflix, Amazon Prime, HBO Max, Hulu. I find the same old nothing. I check social media: Facebook depresses me, Instagram nauseates me, and Twitter … well, I'm not sure what I feel about Twitter. But one thing is clear, I'm still here stuck in this mundane life that hasn't quite lived up to my expectations. No matter how hard I try, I can't resist the pull back to a fictional place where I've been allowed to dream big dreams, to the land of big adventures, a place where anything can happen. Mostly, I'm trying to feel something other than this mind-numbing boredom. Fiction leads to fantasy leads to failure. Then the cycle repeats.

We are thrill-seeking, adrenaline-craving creatures. We recognized it as children on playgrounds where we declared ourselves to be pirates, and princesses, and people in capes trying to save the world. Somewhere along the way we were tamed out of our longings to make a big difference. We were squeezed into boxes of shoulds and do's and expectations. The longer we live, the tighter the box becomes. We convince ourselves that our dreams are too big, our expectations too high, our wants too selfish.

We wake up in the middle of the night aware of just how full our schedules have become and how empty our hearts are. No wonder we're the most depressed and the unhappiest of any generation that has ever lived.

Boredom is one of the reasons men and women seek secret affairs. Men bored with their nonexistent sex lives. Pastors bored with their disappointing calling. Singles bored with their endless waiting. The excitement of an initial secret sexual encounter is intoxicating. The adrenaline of a nameless sexual fantasy becomes an adventure too hard to resist. It's easier to fix boredom with the immediate gratification of an orgasm than to admit how deeply off course your life has become.

Human responses to boredom aren't new to our generation. People have struggled with boredom for centuries. In the Bible narrative, Noah survived the flood but later was so bored he decided to get drunk and spend the night naked where his kids could see him. Lot was so bored after being rescued from

Sodom and Gomorrah that he regularly got drunk enough to get both his daughters pregnant by their careful planning. Solomon filled his hapless life with wives—nine hundred to be exact. And then there's King David. It was boredom that led him to have an affair with Bathsheba that would eventually cost him his family.

Boredom has always paved the way for bad choices. I've spent too much of my life focused on my bad choices and their outcomes. I've found comfort in judging myself too harshly as a form of punishment. I've found temporary relief of my guilt in shaming myself for my sexual perversion. It wasn't until I started accepting the struggle as a means to explore why I was so bored that I found freedom. It's easy to hate the sexual struggle. We want to shun it and compartmentalize it and wish it away. But our sexual struggle, no matter its flavor, tells a story about who we are and who we long to be. Our sexual struggle has a lot to teach us if we are willing to listen.

It wasn't until I gave myself permission to invite the struggle to teach me about my boredom that I started to unravel the negative pattern of behavior I had built.

I was at the beach recently in what can only be described as paradise. The sky a sparkling blue. The sun rippling over the shining waters with the occasional pelican diving in. The pool, because of course there was a pool there too, was filled with perfectly warmed water for frolickers to bathe in. If you were into shells, the sandy shore offered its generous share. If you were into reading, the chaises were there for the taking. If you were into toys, there was an abundance of them scattered around the pool. If people were your jam, you could take your pick. The sun is my thing, so I was deeply content in that moment. Just when I didn't think things could get any better, a kid a few feet away from me said the most infamous words that every kid has ever uttered: "I'm bored!"

How could anyone be bored in a place like this? How can anyone be bored in an era like ours?

Think about it: we're living in a time where we can speak to people by video on a phone. We dreamed of that when I was growing up! We watched the Jetsons do it and never imagined a world where it could actually happen. We can literally get in a metal box and fly halfway across the world. We can order it online and it shows up at our door a few hours later. If we think it, it can happen. We have everything we could ever want at our fingertips, and still we complain about how bored we are.

What I've found about my boredom is that it's internal. While busyness can fill my schedule, boredom has to do with my spirit. Stuff can fill my closets, but boredom is about my soul. As a Christian, I've struggled to reconcile how I can say I believe in a God who fills my longings and still refuse to shake this sense of emptiness.

A few years ago, after I left my church and deconstructed my faith, I stopped talking to God. I didn't stop believing He existed. I just stopped calling home as much. You've been there, I'm sure. You move away from home, the calls home become more infrequent, then one Christmas, you notice that it's been a year since you called your folks. You don't stop believing you have parents; you just lose touch over time.

I lost touch with God because I was mad at Him. I told myself I was mad at God, but beneath the anger, I was hurt. I had grown up believing that God had great plans for me. I had given my life to God hoping that in exchange, He would take me on an adventure. That my life would mean something. That the dreams He would give me would be bigger than the ones I could even dream. I had dreamed that one day I would find the big love, that one day, I would look across the room and just *know*—here was the one I had waited for. I know it sounds idealistic and a little bit naive, but I truly believed that if I honored God with my life, He would fulfill my wildest expectations, and I expected to fall in love in a big way. I wanted it all—a man who still loved me on my bad days, a son who looked like my husband, and a daughter with my attitude in life. I dreamed of laughter at Christmas and staying up late making s'mores in the summer. When I became too cynical to dream about love, I dreamed about the ministry. I dreamed that I would travel around the world leading souls to Christ. I dreamed of making a difference in the world. I dreamed of late-night prayer meetings with other Christian leaders and of revival. I dreamed of more. And I had the verses underlined to support what I dreamed about.

I still do.

Have you ever forgotten a kid at a rest stop? Maybe you've been tempted to! Don't feel bad, it happens to everyone. That's what I felt happened to me. At one point in my life, it felt like God and I stopped at a rest stop on our crazy and awesome adventure to life, but He forgot me back at the overlook and went on without me.

I got bored being at the overlook. At churches all over the place, at least on social media, other Christians were going on exciting adventures with God while I sat around wondering if He was ever going to notice that He'd forgotten me. Other Christians got married, had kids, had kids who got married and had babies—all while I waited for someone to ask me on a first date. Maybe I had bought into the purity culture lie a little over the years.

Christian leaders were the worst. The church that was supposed to be a place where I could unpack some of this baggage was nowhere to be found. I'd never felt the approval of the Christian industry as a whole, and my own church baggage only made me feel more alienated. Other Christian leaders had their revival meetings while I sat back watching from the sidelines, wondering if my number would ever be called.

They—the pastors and Christian leaders—had been invited on the big adventure, and I was stuck in a world full of beaches and toys, but all I could focus on was how miserable my life was.

I was bored to death and angry at a God who had promised a life He wasn't delivering, a God who seemed to have forgotten me. So I filled my time with trivial pursuits. Also, if a pastor ranted against something, it made me want to experience it. The louder they yelled about the sickness of a show, the more intriguing it became. And then when they started falling one by one, I rolled my eyes and said, "I told you so." They're just like the rest of us, bored out of their minds and dying for a way out.

There were two disciples who hung around Jesus during His three years of ministry. James and John. The sons of thunder. They wanted an adventure. They joined Jesus hoping for more. While He didn't disappoint, it wasn't enough for them. One day, they approached Jesus and courageously asked for more. "Grant us," they said, "to sit, one at your right hand and one at your left, in your glory" (Mark 10:37).

They didn't know what they were asking. They didn't get it yet. They were so afraid to be left behind, they wanted shotgun. Jesus wasn't surprised by their request. He did know that they had no idea what they were asking. The others were mad at the brothers. How dare they be so arrogant? How dare they want so much?

I've had time to reflect on Jesus's response while I licked my wounds at the overlook. Tired, bored, alone, and frustrated, when I finally leaned into my sexual struggle and stopped trying to fill the time with an imaginary adventure, I listened.

"Whoever would be first among you must be slave of all. For even the Son of Man came not to be served but to serve, and to give his life as a ransom for many." (Mark 10:44–45).

How have I missed this most of my life?

Are the pastors I've watched to blame for modeling a form of Christianity that elevates those who are more successful, and busier, and more productive than the rest? Is our culture to blame for creating a sense of frenzy and necessary ambition? Or was I to blame for wanting what God already knew would never satisfy me?

We are all thrill-seeking, adrenaline-craving creatures. The most powerful secret we have yet to unfold is that this kind of adventure is found only through dying. I thought I was dying by the overlook wondering what I would do with the rest of my life. I tried to fix my situation with immediate gratification—anything to relieve the boredom.

When I finally stopped long enough to look up, I saw something I never even contemplated was possible. There was Jesus, waiting on the other side of the bench.

It turns out He had been dropped off at the overlook too.

My adventure was just getting started.

# GRAY AREAS

*The gray area, the place between black and white—that's the place where life happens.*
—JUSTIN TIMBERLAKE

THE GUY WHO USED TO BE MY PASTOR—BEFORE HIS leadership demise—was caught gambling in his basement. People in the church were divided. A little more than half of the church members were appalled. How could a pastor gamble? Did he know anything about being a Christian? There were a few brave souls, though, in the back of the room, who were heard mumbling, "Well, the Bible doesn't specifically say that gambling is wrong."

My friend Laurie won half a million dollars on a scratch-off. Ever since she told me, I've wanted to believe that God is okay with gambling. I've tried my luck at three scratch-offs, but every time I lose, I feel like God is trying to tell me something. Gambling, like many other things in our culture, is a gray area. According to the online dictionary, a gray area is a situation that is not clear, or where the rules are not known. Even the word itself is confusing. Is it spelled with an *e* or an *a*? I had to look it up.

I'm obsessed with home remodels and lifestyle Instagram accounts that show before and after pictures and how they got there. The best is how much a color can change a room. Like the color gray, which is really in right now. Did you know that there are 256 different shades of gray to choose from? Most Christians can come up with at least 256 controversial things that we've told ourselves are some shade of gray.

Sometime around the turn of the century, while everyone in the world was worried about Y2K, I sat at my desk searching the world wide web for what the Bible says about masturbation. I had grown up in an environment that warned against premarital sex, and forbade adultery, but I don't recall ever hearing the word *masturbation* in Christian circles. I was too mortified to ask anyone about it, so I had to rely on the Internet. I remember my surprise and relief in finding out that many pastors felt that masturbation was a gray area. I had prescribed to the "God said it, I believe it, that settles it" club, so knowing that the Bible didn't clearly condemn masturbation made me feel like I was let off the hook.

The same logic is used for drinking alcohol, bingeing on Netflix, playing violent video games, and the length of your skirt. Among many other issues.

It's possible to justify just about anything in our modern-day culture with the notion that the Bible doesn't clearly forbid whatever it is we're trying to justify. But sometimes, it takes a lot of mental gymnastics to get there.

I took care of a seventeen-year-old female once whose mom had found out that she was sleeping with her twenty-five-year-old youth group leader. My patient was convinced that because she loved the young man and he loved her back, that God was okay with their relationship. She couldn't fathom a God who might have a different view than hers. She for sure couldn't understand her mom's concern. She told me that Adam and Eve weren't married when they had sex. She told me that the youth leader was planning on marrying her anyway. She told me that they were married in God's eyes. She told me a whole lot of nonsense that the youth leader had told her to justify his sexual abuse of a minor. Sometimes, we don't use the big healthy brain God gave us. We let our feelings do all the thinking.

We can make gray areas out of anything if we try hard enough. But all sins aren't always equal. Some issues aren't as gray as we want them to be.

I've had a close relationship with the Bible my entire life. I grew up in circles that treated the Bible as a rule book. The problem with this strategy is that it falls short. The Bible doesn't address every single issue we will ever face, and some things are not that obvious. The Bible is more than a rule book. It's a picture into God's heart. It's sort of like His Instagram account. You can tell pretty quickly who He is by the snapshots He gives. In fairness, He does give us a lot of snapshots. I imagine if God had a profile on Insta, it would say: "God. Been around forever and not going anywhere for a while. Holy."

Every parent has a set of ground rules for their kids. Don't drink and drive. Don't use drugs. Be home by midnight. You know my parents did. We knew what was expected. We didn't have a list of rules, but we *knew* certain things because we knew *them*. We knew that when they said don't have sex before marriage, they also meant don't do anything that will inevitably lead up to sex either. We knew that breaking any of their rules mattered but that some were a bigger deal than others. Being late for curfew earned us a slap on the wrist, but driving under the influence was unthinkable. Actually, drinking at all in our household was unthinkable, whereas driving under the influence had implications that were even beyond my parents' control.

When push came to shove, it was about whether or not we would honor our parents. It was about respect and understanding. It was relational. My friends didn't have to hold to my parents' curfew or drinking rules, but I did. Well, at least I did if I intended to continue to enjoy my mom's amazing cooking. Even on their most annoying days, I knew that my parents loved me. They had proved themselves good to me over time. It was up to me to decide how I would respond to their love.

For a while I tried to convince myself that I knew God enough to know that He didn't mind the way I was handling my struggle with masturbation. His Word wasn't that clear on the issue anyway. I convinced myself that because what I was doing was a gray area, God would let it slide. Didn't God want me to be happy? Didn't God create sex in the first place? Doesn't God promise to forgive me no matter what anyway?

Have you ever stared at a picture with a friend and seen two completely different things? Lately people who have the same Bible are reaching different conclusions about God than everyone else has for thousands of years. For years, the Golden Rule has been to love God and love others. But lately, some are seeing it a little differently. Even loving God has become a gray area. A lot of people are convinced that loving God really means loving self above all else. Or that loving God means doing what feels good to me no matter the consequences. Or that loving God means pursuing my own happiness above all else as the highest good. But what if *my* highest good ends up hurting everyone else around me?

It's easier to make it a gray area and carry on. We can make gray areas out of anything if we try hard enough.

My friend Nancy was diagnosed with melanoma a few years ago. She hardly told anyone what she was going through, but for a woman who never missed work, we knew something was up. When she came back to work, she told us that she had had bad melanoma and needed aggressive treatment. You would never have guessed it. She looked her usual regal self.

A couple of years passed, and Nancy got ready to retire. She used to come into my office and tell me her dream of waking up early and going to church. She went to church daily, religiously. She dreamed of walking down to the lakeshore in Chicago and just sitting on a bench. That's all she wanted in her retirement.

She lasted a couple of months after retirement. Later, we found out that her melanoma came back in the cruelest fashion just days after retiring. She refused treatment. She had had enough. I was mad at first. Why hadn't she gotten treatment? Shouldn't she have fought for her life? For her family? For us? Eventually, as the pain of losing her lessened, and as I watched my own father go through his own physical struggles in his last few months of life, I saw things a little bit differently. Things aren't always as black and white as we would like them to be.

We pick petty things like gambling and smoking and call them gray areas and spend a lifetime arguing about them with others. We waste our energy on drivel when the *real* gray areas are where we need to invest our energy.

A gray area is whether a woman who wears a hijab and has given her life to Jesus should remove her hijab and risk getting beaten to death by her husband, or keep it even though she feels like doing so is a denial of her newfound life.

A gray area is trying to decide when to stop radiation on your child's brain tumor because he just can't take it anymore, but you can't stand the idea of giving up.

A gray area is when to place a family member in a nursing home because you just don't have the means and ability to care for them anymore, but you promised that you would always be there for them.

In medicine every decision we make boils down to one thing: First, do no harm. It's our oath. It's my guiding light. When I'm not sure what to do, I always weigh the decision against my oath. Will my decision harm or heal? It's critical to identify one thing that clarifies everything when we're wading through the gray.

When it comes to life's gray areas, the best guiding light I've discovered is this question: What's my highest good? What is *your* highest good?

Is your highest good to get what you want, no matter the cost?

Or is your highest good to please God?

The answer should be fairly black and white.

# RELATIVISM

*Pappa don't preach, I'm in trouble deep.*
*Pappa don't preach, I've been losing sleep.*
—MADONNA

*Judge not, that ye be not judged.*
—JESUS

I DO NOT CLAIM TO BE A LESBIAN, NOR DO I STRUGGLE with my sexual identity, but I can assure you that the lines can become blurred when it comes to our sexual struggles and desires as humans. The first time I felt attracted to a woman happened in the context of late-night browsing on the web. I was lonely and hurting and reeling from my breakup with my church and all things Christian institution. The next day, I emailed a dear friend whom I knew would understand, and I confessed my problem. Later, I asked my therapist if she thought I was a lesbian. It would be much more convenient to position this incident prior to my salvation where I could scrub it away by the blood of Jesus and move on with an unassuming heterosexual life.

I catch myself wanting to soften the blow of what I just confessed by telling you that studies have proven that straight women regularly show patterns of same-sex attraction when viewing porn. I also want to make you think better of me by telling you that I can count on one hand the times I've struggled with this, but it sounds contrived even to my own ears. Besides, I've committed to telling you my story as honestly as I can.

My nephew Sam, age nine, has warned me this is the chapter that might get me canceled by Amazon. What's ironic is that there is a higher risk of me getting canceled by Christians than there is by the LGBTQ community. I have tried my best to skip this conversation, but how can I talk about sex in today's world without talking about same-sex attraction?

What makes a sin too perverted to handle? Does sin become worse when it moves from the mind to the eye? Does it become worse when it breaks the marriage bond versus when it happens in single-ness? Does it have an age limit where it becomes unacceptable? Are certain acts okay whereas others cross the line? Is sex in the context of a movie with a proper plot more acceptable than sex on a website? Is it worse when a pastor falls to sexual sin than when the rest of us do?

On the one hand, the culture at large is quick to cancel anyone who disagrees with their sexual world-view. On the other hand, the conservative Christian community, of which I am a part, is quick to cancel anyone who isn't dogmatically and vehemently staunch in their opposition of the culture. Yet I hold this topic with a sacred reverence and care. I have many friends who are in same-sex relationships. One of my very best friends is married to a woman. I want to honor her and others in the LGBTQ world because they are indeed made in the image of God and are brothers, sisters, mothers, daughters, friends, and relatives. On the other hand, I cannot deny what I believe is the truth about sex and sexuality.

This chapter is not an indictment against homosexuality. Rather, it is a call to those of us who call ourselves followers of Jesus to turn from our own hypocrisy and take the log out of our own eye before meddling with our neighbor's vision. I have written about my broken sexuality in as much honesty as I can so far, and by God's grace, I'll continue to do so.

Relativism can become dizzying.

All I know is that one day I was reading G-rated love stories, and the next day I was watching mainstream shows on HBO Max heavy with all kinds of nonbiblical sexual content—and enjoying them. Eventually I crossed another line or two that I never thought I would. I consider it only God's mercy that my sexual struggle has been on the unseen pages of my brain and imagination. In the secret recesses of my cranium, I have crossed lines that even I'm afraid to share publicly on these pages.

For as far back as I can remember, I've looked to others, especially their failures and inadequacies, as a means to boost my own self-confidence. In elementary school, it was in our grades and our recess activities that we compared ourselves to others. Nowadays, it's social media that offers a look at other people's lives and a window for us to feel better about ourselves. When I struggle with my weight, I scan through social media for others who are fatter than I am, and suddenly my eating choices aren't as bad as I thought they were. When I struggle with my singleness, I'm encouraged by the breakup of a marriage or a dating relationship. When I struggle with my performance in my ministry, I can't help but feel smug whenever I hear that someone else's performance was even worse than mine.

And when I struggle with my sexual baggage, I have been oddly reassured when hearing of the massive sexual failures of so many Christian leaders. The more excruciating the details of a scandal, the better I feel about myself. I'm not that bad after all, am I? There are many out there who are much worse than me. It's reassuring to think that we're not as bad as everybody else, isn't it? But it's a poor strategy in the long haul. When we compare ourselves to others, it feels good for a while. But here's the rub: it doesn't change who we are. I might find temporary safety in finding myself less sinful than my neighbor, but I am just as guilty and just as broken inside.

No wonder I need a Savior.

I don't know when Christians became experts at grading sin, but experts we have become. Like the Pharisees before us, we have positioned ourselves as our culture's moral police. We want to whip everyone around us into place with our vitriol, all the while ignoring our own inconsistent patterns and hypocrisy. Some have called it our necessary calling. I disagree. Our necessary calling is to holiness, and we are falling short by a mile.

Logic invites us to accept that sin should indeed be graded. Raping someone is worse than gossiping about someone. Stealing ten dollars from my mom's wallet when I was eight was bad, but cheating on my taxes as an adult would land me in jail. It's common sense. It's also biblical. I hold to a biblical worldview that teaches that all sin big or small is mortal, but that same worldview teaches me that all sin is not equal in its consequences and in relation to others. Jesus mentions the unpardonable sin in the Gospels. James, the brother of Jesus, writes that those who know more are held to higher accountability. Premeditated sin carries greater consequence. Certain sins cry out to God and demand justice on behalf of the marginalized.

The fact that God grades sin should be reassuring to us, but sometimes, it can be inconvenient to the things that we crave.

I wish I could tell you that as a follower of Jesus, I have had a natural loathing of all things sexual outside of the boundaries of what God commands, but that would not be truthful. I enjoy sex in many of its formats. I have enjoyed movies with sexual content and scenes, be it premarital intercourse or adulterous affairs. My bend is to favor my flesh over my spirit. It has been hard work to crucify the flesh. Some days have been more successful than others.

Most Christians reading this are horrified. You have already canceled me in your minds. "Repent!" you're crying out. "Change!" Don't worry. You haven't told me anything I haven't already told myself a million times over. I *am* a hypocrite even when I try to convince myself that I am not. Yet I have found solace in the arms of Jesus over and over again. I don't believe I'm alone in this struggle. Statistically speaking, while the church throws stones at same-sex attraction, porn is rampant in the church pews. We cheat. We divorce. We lust. We speak lewdly. We covet. We lie. We assume God will put up with our sin. We might not flaunt it as flagrantly as others, but we are just as guilty inside. We resort to grading sin because it helps alleviate the guilt of our own sin. While sin can and must be graded, I have found myself busy enough pursuing my own personal holiness to throw stones at others.

It's been fascinating to watch conservative Christians in the last decade handle issues related to same-sex attraction and gender identity. We are much like the Pharisees who were proud to throw the woman caught in adultery at the feet of Jesus demanding judgment. The result wasn't what they expected. Instead of condemning the woman, who was indeed guilty of sexual sin, Jesus had nothing but compassion for the woman. He did indict the Pharisees that day though. He knew that they weren't as holy as they wanted everyone to think they were.

It's fascinating to me that in the Old Testament, there are two scary incidents where God kills two of His people in judgment. The first was Korah, in Numbers 16:1–40. He conspired against Moses. His punishment was death. The second was Uzzah in 2 Samuel 6:1–7. He touched the ark of the covenant when he wasn't supposed to. Neither were sexual sinners. Both were punished far more severely than many of us would admit they deserved.

Perhaps God sees things differently than we do.

God's chosen people are certainly no sex saints. Judah, the son of Jacob who would later carry the line of Christ, was guilty of prostitution with his own daughter-in-law. David, the man after God's own heart, was guilty of committing adultery. Samson was unequally yoked with women who worshipped false gods. Solomon, the son of David, was a severe and serial polygamist with nine hundred wives. Rahab was a prostitute. Reuben committed incest by sleeping with his father's wife. The list of sexual deviants is long.

The people of God have always been a sexual mess. We are in good company that way. I have found great hope in these facts. I have found great hope in God's mercies.

I am convinced that God in His Word, the Bible, teaches that the only sexual relationship ordained by God is between a man and his wife in the context of marriage. But I am equally convinced that Christians have been guilty of moral relativism as it pertains to sexual sin. In doing so, we have lost the culture war and alienated our loved ones.

Could we have done things differently? Could Christians who uphold the truth of God's Word have handled the conversation on sexual identity and same-sex attraction better? More lovingly? Would it have changed the outcome of our culture's perception on these topics if we had? Could Christians have had a stronger influence on other people's lives by living more honestly in our own bedrooms?

Even though I am a fifty-year-old virgin, I have served as a sex therapist for my many patients in the course of my medical practice these twenty-five years. Patients regularly ask me about their sex lives and the consequences of their sexual choices. They long to avoid the negative consequences of their choices but can't seem to control their actions. Once in a while I'm asked my personal opinion on their sexual practices. When I'm offered this privilege,

I have chosen to speak both as honestly but as compassionately as I am able to. I give my thoughts carefully, aware of the holiness of the moment. If my opinion is not sought, I do not impose it.

Why is it understandable for me to have compassion and a sense of professional respect with my patients, while we get a free pass to crucify our neighbors for their choices in real life?

We idolize sex in our culture. We treat sex as if it's a right and not a gift. I can understand when those who don't know God and don't hold to a biblical worldview hold sexual fulfillment as their highest possible attainment. The hypocrisy of today's Christian, myself included more often than I care to admit, is that we have bought into the lie that our sexual fulfillment is our number-one priority. Singles long to have sex. Married people long to have better sex. Our addiction to porn and our pursuit of illicit affairs and our rate of divorce and our comfort with divorce only attest to the fact that we have a sex problem in the church. If we spent half the time focused on our own holiness as we do trying to change the culture back to its Puritan ways, our words might have more impact.

At the heart of my sexual struggle has always been the invitation to choose God over self. Each time I have turned to sexual perversion and sin for comfort has been one more time that I have turned away from God and His way. Each time I have sought comfort in temporary gratification has been my idolizing my sexual desires over God.

The longer I live, the more I am convinced that the only victory in our cultural war for purity will not take place in Washington, DC, or in Hollywood, but in the very secret place of our own hearts. Church, until we surrender our own sexual wants and seek God, and until we learn that holiness starts in the secret places of our bedrooms, we are doomed to fail in winning the culture for Christ.

Everything else is only relative.

# MASTURBATING

*I chase the moment that when I had it I felt alive*
*But now that the thrill is gone*
*I feel dead inside*
—ANDY MINEO

FOR A LONG WHILE I PRETENDED NOT TO NOTICE THAT
even though I had given my life to Jesus, I was
spending it doing whatever the heck I wanted to.
During the day I acted like a Christian, but late at
night, I focused on pleasing myself.

Anytime I felt the surge of guilt rise, I shoved
it back down with some soothing facts: the Bible
doesn't say anywhere that masturbating is a sin. A lot
of pastors don't agree that masturbating is a sin. I'm
too old to worry about the effects of masturbating
on my future love life. But my ace in the hole was
that when all was said and done, I was not hurting
anyone with what I was doing anyway.

I started masturbating when I was ten. Back then
I was driven by my hormones. Later in life, I found
it a lot easier to take care of business than suffer
through today's dating world in order to find the
right man to marry. I don't remember the details of
how it all started, just that one day I was living alone,
and the next day masturbation had moved into my
house for good. I hadn't been sexually abused. I wasn't
a neglected kid. I didn't have parents that didn't care
about me. I just started a habit that pretty soon I was
hooked on.

Over the years I've had friends come and go, I've changed jobs, and I've moved cities and houses, but the two things that have remained constants in my life are God and masturbation. I've convinced myself that the two can coexist. We can convince ourselves of anything when we try hard enough.

Did you know that the word *masturbate* comes from the word *manstupare*, a compound of *manu*, which means "hand" and *stuprare*, meaning to "defile" oneself, related to *stupere*, which means "to be stunned, stupefied."[20] Translated literally, an interpretation of "masturbation" could well be, "To make one stupid by hand."

It's quite fitting on many levels, don't you think? Ironically, as sexually comfortable as we have become as a culture, this topic is still considered untouchable in most Christian circles.

When I was thirteen, I spent a month away at a summer camp in France to get better at speaking French and for a short respite from the civil war in Beirut, the city I was born in. It was my tough luck that I got my first period thousands of miles away from home and the reassuring presence of my mother. I was emotionally unprepared for dealing with something as natural as getting my period in that setting. I found my counselor and, choking back tears, awkwardly asked her for a tampon. I'm still scarred by the experience.

In the same way that discussing your period in public company is awkward, and in the same way that reviewing your bowel habits with others is off limits, talking about how often you masturbate and why is largely avoided in proper Christian culture. Nobody likes to talk about it, but almost everyone is doing it.

I wish someone had talked to me about masturbation when I was ten. I might have avoided a lot of mental gymnastics trying to reconcile who I was with who I wanted to be. Lately, I've become more ambivalent about masturbation. It's stolen so much from me already that I'd rather not give it another minute of my time. Yet an honest conversation about masturbation is why some of you even bought this book, so for better or for worse, we're going to sit down and do this.

When you stop and think about it, masturbation is the Amazon Prime of sex acts. It's the ultimate Gen Z vice. It's individualistic, socially conscious, and pragmatic. Also, it doesn't really hurt anyone. That single Christians masturbate is the most obvious foregone conclusion that most Christians try not to think too much about. The idea that Christian singles can be exposed to the amount of sex in our current culture and not have to find release somewhere is naive at best. Christian culture tends to be much more open to the idea of married people masturbating, which seems mean to me. Still, when it comes to helping people deal with this particular sexual struggle, the church has by and large feigned ignorance to the extent of the problem.

I have been writing about masturbation for more than a decade. If I have any regrets about how I've communicated on this topic, it's that I haven't been clear enough with my words. It reminds me of when I was first starting out in medicine. I used to dance around my words, afraid of saying the wrong thing. I had to develop confidence in myself first before I became effective at helping others. After twenty years in the ER, I now know that the more confusing the disease is, the simpler my language must be. We can't tiptoe around certain topics.

I don't remember the first time I masturbated, but I do know that it took me at least thirty years before I could comfortably say the word out loud—*masturbate. Masturbation, masturbator.* Did you know that there are over five hundred euphemisms for the word *masturbation*? Maybe I'm not the only one who struggles with saying the word out loud. What I do remember is the guilt, the shame, the self-loathing, the struggle, the thousands of journal entries, and the sense of defeat that would plague me for years because of the word. I remember my repeated confessions to God and the promises I made Him that I'd never do it again. I remember the joy I've felt when

I've temporarily managed to kick masturbation out of my house. Sooner or later, like an adult child who can't help making their way back home, masturbation would come knocking on my door, and I, like the resigned parent who feels like they have no choice, would open the door and let them in.

In my late twenties, I scoured every article that I could find on the topic of masturbation. If a pastor had written it, I read it. I learned that masturbation might have a negative impact on one's future married life. Whether this is true or not, I cannot tell, but it scared me enough to curb the habit for a while, but that didn't last very long. I spent so much time asking God to help me to stop that the angels went on strike. My prayers have remained largely unanswered. A dear friend of mine challenges me, "Don't pray if you're not willing to act." She's right, but some days my pain is too present to act. I have to work myself up to act. It's never easy. That same friend reminds me that her point isn't, "Don't pray if you don't act," but that honest prayers come with a willingness to act in accordance with God's revealed will. Instead of focusing my prayers on the outcome I wish would happen, my focus should shift to praying for God's will: for my heart to remain soft and willing to repent and for my longings to align to His. Maybe my prayers are being answered after all.

In time, I did find encouraging bits of information though. Christian leaders and pastors are in fact
divided on the topic of masturbation. While some
are quick to condemn it, many are equivocal about
it. Everyone agrees that nowhere in the Bible does
God directly forbid the act. But everyone also agrees
that lust and pornography are wrong and are almost
always associated with the act of masturbation. I
can attest that the latter is true. The conclusion for
most pastors, it seems, is that if you can masturbate
without lusting, you're good. This is in fact possible,
though not as much fun.

There is one biblical reference that pastors
occasionally point to when discussing the negative merits of masturbation. It's the story of a man
named Onan in Genesis 38.

Here's how it goes: Judah had three sons—Er,
Onan, and Shelah. Er married Tamar, then Er died.
Judah told his second-born son, Onan, to carry out
his family duty and get Tamar pregnant. This was
the norm back in those days. Onan was sly. He didn't
want to father a son on behalf of his brother, so while
he did agree to sleep with Tamar, he refused to seal
the deal. The exact words are like this: "But Onan
knew that the offspring would not be his. So whenever he went in to his brother's wife he would waste
the semen on the ground, so as not to give offspring
to his brother" (Genesis 38:9).

As a physician, I am puzzled by the conclusion of some Christians that Onan was masturbating in this incident. Anyone with a basic knowledge of sexual intercourse can conclude that Onan was ejaculating outside of the vaginal canal as a means of avoiding reproduction. They didn't have birth control or condoms in those days, so a guy had to do what he had to do. In a way, you can say Onan was practicing safe sex. Some people still use this method for birth control today.

The point I'm trying to make is that there is indeed no direct Bible passage that specifically forbids masturbation. I have never been as reassured by this as I'd like to be. Even though the Academy of Pediatrics tells me it's normal,[21] and the sexual culture at large advises me to enjoy it, and the church reassures me that God doesn't directly forbid it, over the years I have come to understand that masturbation is too often a sign that something is off in my life.

I grew up dreaming of radical obedience to Jesus. I was happily willing to lay down my life and sacrifice everything to make Jesus known. Well ... almost everything. I was so sure that my teenage phase of masturbation would be just that, a phase. When it morphed into a habit, I was concerned. When it showed signs of a habit I couldn't shake, I became discouraged. Some days my feelings border on despair. Why can't I change? Why can't I get my act together? I've been tempted to give in to self-loathing. I have lived a large portion of my life with a gnawing sense of unworthiness over my sexual struggle. I live with a constant sense of hypocrisy alleviated by the seasons in my life where I've been clean, so to speak.

What might have saved my life and ministry was an obscure article written by John Piper back in the early eighties called "Missions and Masturbation"[22] and a sermon he gave at Passion 2007 in Atlanta, Georgia. He said, "The great tragedy is not mainly masturbation or fornication or acting like a peeping Tom (or curious Cathy) on the Internet. *The tragedy is that Satan uses the guilt of these failures to strip you of every radical dream you ever had,* or might have, and in its place give you a happy, safe, secure, American life of superficial pleasures until you die in your lakeside rocking chair, wrinkled and useless, leaving a big fat inheritance to your middle-aged children to confirm them in their worldliness. That's the main tragedy."[23]

I have almost quit. I still tell myself I deserve to quit. But I'm still here by God's grace.

I refuse to be stripped of my God-given dreams. I refuse to give in to my worst vices, no matter how long it takes for me to subdue them.

Sometimes I try to justify my actions because, after all, God is the one who created me this way.

He's the one who's given me my sexual impulses. I recently read a very popular author whose perspective of what happened in Eden was a sign of strength for Eve. I refuse to pretend that grabbing the proverbial fruit in the garden is an act of courage and declaration of how strong I am. I know the truth. I know that each time I grab for the fruit is an act of rebellion against God.

I used to wonder if masturbation was the unpardonable sin. It's not. I've wanted to assume that masturbation was Paul's thorn in the flesh. I don't believe it was. I've worried about whether masturbation will ruin my married sex life. Jury is still out on that one.

I am learning to see myself as more than my worst sin. I am learning to listen to the voice inside me—the one that knows that though masturbation is permissible for some, it's not okay for me. It comes with too many caveats and pathways to perversion.

I am learning to believe that I am just as loved by God on my worst day as I am on my best, and that even if I struggle until the day I die, God still loves me completely. I am slowly learning to value that what He thinks of me is far more important than what everyone else in the world does. His love has given me confidence. It's why I am able to speak more clearly about this here.

I am learning, and this is the hardest, to turn to Him when I am hurting instead of turning to myself. It's hard because over the years, I've blamed God for a lot of my baggage. It's hard because I can't see God and sometimes it feels like I'm talking to myself. It's hard because most people generally laugh at the idea that God cares about whether humans masturbate, and it's tempting to side with them. It's tempting to trivialize the whole thing. It's hard because it's easy to make sex about anatomy and release, but I'm learning that sex is a lot more about connection and intimacy. You can have all the orgasms in the world and still not feel satisfied because your soul is missing. I'm learning that it's my soul God longs for.

For a long while, I pretended not to notice that even though I had given my life to Jesus, I was spending it doing whatever the heck I wanted to.

Even if I die trying, it's time for this to change.

# SHAME

*Don't forget that I'm human, don't forget that I'm real.*
—Justin Bieber

I GOT TIRED OF FEELING ASHAMED. SHAME CLUNG TO me, always right there underneath the surface. I couldn't shake it no matter how hard I tried—the feeling that I'm less than, not enough. I was ashamed that I couldn't stop myself from feeling this way.

I say that I love God more than anything, yet again and again I have proven through my actions that I'm a liar—that I love one thing more: myself. That makes me feel ashamed. I'm ashamed that even though I know that God has forgiven me through Christ's death on the cross, for the life of me I can't stop the shame, and I can't shape up like other Christians and let the cross be the cross and me be happy, or joyful, or both.

Being ashamed makes me angry. I'm mad at everything all the time. I'm mad at myself the most for not being able to move past the shame. I'm mad at God for not helping me, not fixing me. I'm mad at the church for not understanding me. I'm mad because no matter what I do, how hard I try, it never seems to be enough. I'm mad that I don't know how to get out of this place I'm in. It's a lot more work to dig past your anger to your shame, but I've found the connection between these two emotions is too real to ignore.

They say that every person's shame tells a story. What's my story? Not the raunchy details of my sexual struggles, but the real me. What story does my shame tell about me?

Once, when I was nine, I overheard my ballet teacher tell my mom that I had gained weight and would never have the body of a ballerina. She saw no future for me in dance. It's actually quite funny, because anyone who knows me knows that my weight is the last thing that stood in the way of my future as a ballerina, but back then, I didn't laugh. I got this sick feeling in my stomach instead. I looked around to see if anyone had heard her. I stopped breathing. I felt nauseated and dizzy and weak. I wanted to make a hole in the ground and stay in it. I wanted to hide. I've been ashamed about my body ever since. The saddest part was that I had had emergency surgery just a few weeks prior to that conversation and had my abdomen cut open all the way across. That was my first time back to ballet since the surgery. That I was even at ballet was a miracle in and of itself. My weight should have been the last thing on my teacher's mind, but still ... the memory is imprinted in my mind forever, shaping the way that I feel about myself.

A few years later, I'm at a summer college thing and have been asked to do a mandatory pre-employment physical. The old gruff doctor gets me on the scale. I remember every detail, even the smell in the room. The scale reads 145 pounds. The doctor doesn't look up. He jots the number on the chart, then makes the declaration: "You're fat. You need to lose weight."

There are some things we can know in the head but have a really hard time translating into real life. How I view myself is one of those things. Any genius can conclude that I have been deeply affected and shaped by the conclusions of a perfectionist ballerina and an ignorant doctor, but for better or for worse, these statements have shaped my shame.

I have lived most of my life ashamed—not just in my body image but in a variety of ways. Shame has relentlessly pursued me.

Shame is failing my first Pediatric ER boards and having to show up to the ER the next day and act like everything was normal.

Shame is sitting on a couch next to my best friend and being told that he didn't feel the same way about me that I felt about him.

Shame is adult acne.

Shame is still being single at fifty.

Shame is not having a date for over ten years and counting.

Shame is that the best sexual experience I've had so far happened on my own.

The list goes on. No matter how hard I've tried to channel my inner Brené Brown and try to understand and overcome my shame, it's been a long and arduous road. I haven't had a lot of compassion for myself on this journey.

When I look at myself, I see every inadequacy, every mistake, every failure, every extra pound, every skin blemish, every blunder and miscalculation, and conclude that I'm not enough. Like anyone else who wrestles with shame, my shame has driven me to a life of perfectionism. I have worked harder than anyone else, tried harder than anyone else, and like a kid at the fair banging on the Whac-A-Mole, I have tried to defeat shame's voice each time it rears its ugly head.

But shame's voice is louder. On most days, it feels like it's winning.

Almost anyone who has struggled with pornography and sexual sin in any of its forms understands shame. It's hard to talk about the struggle, and when we do, it's impossible not to shift around and avoid eye contact. Our answers are vague, never quite telling the entire story. Heads droop, bodies hunch over, and faces feel flushed. It's easier to hide than to endure those feelings. It's easier to hide than to let someone else see who we really are.

While it's easy to understand that a person's sexual struggle is the cause of shame, it's actually been well documented that when it comes to shame and pornography, shame is also a key driver in porn use for both men and women. We are always looking for evidence to confirm the belief that we are as unlovable and deficient as we feel we are. Maybe even worse. We don't deserve love and acceptance. Our sexual struggle is one more sign of how sick we are.

On my bad days, when all I can think about are my failures, and my defects, and how unwanted I am, it feels good to feel bad about myself. It's easier to feel bad than to try and convince myself of the truth—that I am loved unconditionally, broken and all.

So much shame is influenced by our values, our expectations, and our cultural standards. For a Syrian refugee woman, where marriage is considered the highest value, being single invites deep shame. In an Indian home, where education and accomplishment are highly valued, a child dropping out of college may feel shameful. In a Christian home, where sexual purity is prized, shame oozes out of a struggle with pornography. Ironically, most people in the West who don't hold to a Christian worldview can watch porn without any remorse or regret. Porn is as natural as breathing.

It's possible to feel shame without being guilty of wrongdoing. The kid who drops out of college hasn't done anything wrong but still carries the shame of his family's disappointment. The Syrian woman who hasn't been married hasn't done anything wrong but feels the burden of her unwantedness. A victim of sexual abuse isn't guilty but carries the unfathomable weight of unwanted and uninvited shame.

It's also possible to be guilty without feeling ashamed. The couple who claims to not believe in God and is living together before marriage is guilty of fornication though they may carry no shame yet. They don't yet recognize the God who judges them.

Most commonly people feel shame and guilt at the same time. This has been my plight. I know my guilt well and I feel my shame deeply. I get the difference. Guilt tells me I did something wrong, while shame reminds me that something is wrong with me, but the two get muddled in my mind.

When it comes to my guilt, I am aware and grateful that Jesus has paid the price for my sin when He was crucified on the cross. It's shame that paralyzes me. It's shame that isolates me. It's shame that alienates me at times even from God. It's easier to hide than to let Him see me. As if He didn't know me already. But He's been looking for those of us who are hiding for a while.

Adam and Eve were guilty and they were ashamed. So they hid from God. But God looked for them and He found them.

King David was guilty and he was ashamed. So he hid the truth from God. But God looked for him and He found him.

The Samaritan woman was guilty and she was ashamed. So she hid in the anonymity of a noontime well. But God looked for her and He found her.

Peter was guilty and he was ashamed. So he hid in the distraction of his fishing boat. But God looked for him and He found him.

The same story repeats itself through the pages of Scripture. We are all guilty and ashamed. So we hide. We hide in our jobs. We hide in our homes. We hide in our addictions. We hide in our appearances. We hide in our perfect Christian behavior. God still looks for us, and He finds us. He sees us. He knows us.

It's easier to punish myself by continuing to struggle than to give in to the goodness of God. It takes humility to admit that there is nothing that can be done about my guilt and shame outside of Jesus Christ. No amount of perfectionist effort will fix me. No amount of trying hard will heal me.

I'm not much different than the woman with the bleeding disorder back in Jesus's days. She had tried to find healing anyway she could. She eventually ran out of resources. At the end, there was only Jesus. After reaching out to touch the hem of His robe, He looked for her. And He found her. When He called on her to expose herself, she had to choose: let her shame paralyze her, or step into the light.

She chose to be vulnerable. She chose the light.

I found a mouse in my house one day. It was barely alive right inside the sill of my bathroom. I almost crushed it by accident. I freaked out. Then I grabbed the fortunately empty laundry basket and covered the mouse with it. I called my realtor, who much to his dismay is my brother-in-law, and told him that if he didn't come over to my house in the next five minutes to get rid of the dying mouse, I would do something crazy. While waiting for my brother-in-law, I promised myself that I would tell absolutely no one about the mouse. How embarrassing would it be if they knew? What would that say about me? Would it affect the value of my house if I tried to sell the house with the mouse in it? I didn't want to know.

My brother-in-law must have believed me because he showed up exactly five minutes later. I was beside myself by then. We took care of the mouse, and by we, I mean he. And then I tried to move on.

I kept my secret for as long as I could, but my best friend, Tina, was due to spend the night later in the week and I was worried she'd find out. What if another mouse showed up dead when she came? After debating the best next step, I decided to confess my little secret. I couldn't find the right words so I texted her the best picture of the baby mouse I could find and sent it without comment.

I held my breath and waited while she responded. A few seconds later, her response came through. She sent me a picture of a mouse far uglier and bigger than mine. It turned out that Tina had had to deal with her share of mice problems too. Instead of judging me, Tina understood.

Brené Brown says, "If we can share our story with someone who responds with empathy and understanding, shame can't survive."[24] I know that to be true. While the gospel assures us that our guilt and our shame are forgiven in Christ on the cross, the best way to get through shame is by talking about it. Secrecy is the soil in which shame grows. But sharing our shame requires us to be vulnerable, and vulnerability is risky. It's the hardest thing some of us will ever have to do.

Even more tragic is that most Christian leaders and pastors don't have the luxury of sharing their story. They carry their shame knowing that any amount of vulnerability in the area of sexual struggle might cost them their jobs. They have too much to lose by coming clean. So they choose to go on hiding. But you can hide for only so long. Sooner or later, if there is a dead mouse in your house, the stench will become too obvious.

I had been going to therapy for several weeks already and still didn't have the guts to bring up the main reason I was there. Each time I tried to bring it up, I felt a tightness in my chest. What if she can't stand to look at me if I tell her? In time though, I ran out of things to say. I had to decide. Would I stay hidden in the darkness paralyzed by my shame, or would I step into the light? I was paying her to listen, so there was that. And she *had* promised confidentiality, so what did I have to lose, really? Just my pride. Always that pride. Would she still like me after I told her? Would she respect me? Before I knew it, the words tumbled out. Then there was nothing left to hide.

They say that the only way to resolve shame is to talk about it.

These days, I'm not as mad as I used to be.

# BREATHE

*These days my waves get lost in the oceans.*
*Seven billion swimmers,*
*man I'm going through the motions....*
*If there's so many people here, then why am I so lonely?*
—ONE REPUBLIC

IT'S EIGHT O'CLOCK ON A SUNDAY MORNING. BY THE time you're up and have had your second cup of coffee, I'll have seen over fifty patients. There's no sabbath for me. I haven't taken a day off in 2,560 days. I've written multiple books, recorded hundreds of podcasts, started a nonprofit, traveled to more cities than I can remember, spoken at conferences, and produced a daily minute on the radio. You might be horrified to hear it. Most people are pretty impressed.

I'm the queen of hustle.

I came out of the womb hustling. I skipped kindergarten, graduated high school at sixteen, and completed medical school at twenty-four. I finished my pediatric residency at twenty-seven and my fellowship in pediatric emergency medicine at thirty. Wrapped up my MBA from one of the top three business schools in the country by thirty-five. I bought my first house at twenty-eight and a few more since. I will have paid off all my mortgages by the time you read this book.

I'm not bragging. Just sharing the facts.

I sat in my therapist's office on a Thursday afternoon trying to make sense of it all. She told me we would try something different that day. "Close your eyes. I'm going to play a song. Just listen for a minute," she instructed me. I'm not one of those people who is comfortable with exercises like that. I smirked but did as she said. She played an old song by Fernando Ortega, a quiet song. I lasted a minute. Then I started sobbing. It was a song I knew from days long gone, before the hustle took over. It was a song that reminded me that life is more than the number of patients that you see, or the number of zeros on your checking account. Mostly, it was a song about silence. It was a song about God.

No one ever told me that the hustle would be so lonely. Or maybe they did and I didn't listen.

I used to drink my coffee black. Almost my entire life, no matter the time of day, if I had a cup of coffee, it was black. One day I noticed that I never drank more than a couple of sips of the coffee. It occurred to me that I didn't like it. I did the unthinkable. I poured cream in my coffee and tried it. I loved it. So at the ripe old age of forty-nine, I began drinking my coffee with cream in it, and I love it. It's changed my life.

Did you ever consider that we might not be doing things the right way? That just because we've done it the same way a million times before doesn't mean it's the best way?

Hustle is the holy grail of our culture. We take pride in working 24/7/365. We work hard every single day come rain or shine. We're mad at Chick-fil-A for closing on Sundays. We have only one life, and we're going to milk every minute out of it even if it kills us.

And it is killing some of us, or at the very least it's killing our marriages. And our churches. And our communities. And our souls.

The problem with hustle is that it never stops. You hustle to get there, but what you don't know is that the hustle doesn't stop when you get there. It's just getting started. The hustle never stops. You buy a house, then need a second. You get your Rolex, but there's a better one out there. You write a book only to start worrying about the next one. Your Insta post blows up, now you need another viral post. And so on and so forth.

If there's anything worse than hustle, it's Christian hustle. Christian hustle culture is poison, the antithesis of what it means to be a Christian. All over America are pastors and leaders who are caught up in the hustle. For them it's filling seats in auditoriums, getting invited to speak at conferences, changing the world for Jesus one bestseller at a time. Slowly but surely, the hustle is sucking the Spirit out of us.

Hustling is my jam and it's been really, really lonely.

When I was in medical school, we ran the year in blocks. At the end of every block was a series of exams. It felt like hell, leading up to the end of a block. After the exams were over, everyone got together at a local bar where they would drink their brains out. I watched from the sidelines, too Christian to participate but aware that it was generally agreed on that we deserved to let loose after all the hard work. We could do anything we wanted to because we'd earned it. Letting loose was the reward for the hustle. Self-indulgence the answer to our pain.

Later I worked in the emergency department of a major metropolitan city. We had the same ritual after a big night at work. The crazier the shift, the more we felt entitled to let off some steam. We deserved it. We needed it. After a couple of hours, everyone scattered home half drunk and numb enough to go to sleep for a few hours.

That's the problem with hustle. It's a pressure cooker that eventually explodes. What's left after the explosion is a whole lot of rubble.

Turning to sex for release is a tale as old as time. We've seen it in every action movie. The hero comes back home and makes a beeline to his waiting woman. Only in today's world, the pastor who is hustling comes home to a woman who is home-schooling the kids and moving the laundry from the washer to the dryer and getting dinner ready for everyone. The last thing on her mind is sex. So the hero turns elsewhere for release. He needs the applause of someone, anyone. He needs affirmation. He needs attention. Mostly, though, he needs love. He needs intimacy. He just doesn't know how to ask for it. He doesn't know what it looks like. All he's ever been taught is hustle and release. Then repeat.

Hustle. Release. Repeat.

For years I'd told myself that I deserved release because I worked so hard. I deserved the break. The busier I became, the less margin I had for living. I lost the ability to connect with others in real life. I didn't have time to be vulnerable. I had too much to do and barely enough time. The pressure kept building. Instead of feeling like a hero, I felt like an unseen victim. I had chosen a life of service, and service had become my prison. It was killing my soul.

Then out of the blue I was sidelined. In the middle of my Christian hustle, I was benched. You can take what I'm about to tell you with a grain of salt. Some of our struggles sound flimsy when we speak them out loud, and my experience with Christian hustle is one of them. Because I had grown up in the evangel-ical megachurch culture, I bought into the Christian hustle hook, line, and sinker. Instead of embracing

God's vision for success and significance, there was a time in my life not that long ago that I bought into the idea that bigger was better and that God's favor meant more—more followers, more book sales, more invitations to speak, more influence. Even though I was saving lives in the emergency department during this somewhat embarrassing season, my Christian culture and leadership were modeling a way that elevated their work as the real work and their successes as the epitome of God's favor.

That season messed with my thinking big-time. It messed with me because while all my peers seemed to be getting better book deals and bigger audiences to evangelize, I felt overlooked. While all my peers were invited to the proverbial Christian table, I was left to fend for myself having walked away from my megachurch disappointment. While others lived the miracle of the feeding of the five thousand, I was the Phoenician woman in the Gospel of Mark begging to eat the crumbs left for the dogs beneath the table (Mark 7:28). It was the worst thing that could happen to me. I felt stabbed in the gut by God. I wondered if I was being punished for masturbating too much. COVID ended up being a lucky break for me. It gave me a good explanation for the crisis that had already hit me. It was this crisis that landed me in therapy. Up to that point I wasn't the kind of person who did therapy. I rolled my eyes at people who did. I was

too busy hustling to need anyone's help. Now, I was
the one who needed help making sense of my crisis:
Instead of a bigger platform, I had plateaued. Instead
of more speaking invitations like the other authors I
knew, I fizzled. Instead of bigger stages, all I had was
a bigger headache. It was a disaster.

I went down kicking and screaming.

Have you ever watched a five-year-old throw a
tantrum? It's awful. There's huffing and puffing and
yelling and moaning. Then even after the battle is
clearly lost, they can't stop stewing. That was me in
a nutshell. I stewed for a long while. It was an act of
God's grace. But it took me a while to see it.

I was like an addict going through withdrawal. I
had been addicted to hustle, using it as a pass for
bad behavior. When the dust settled, I started to
notice the ache.

The ache. I waited for it to pass. I tried to numb
the ache with release. I hid in a world of sexual
fantasy. I tiptoed into more and more titillating
content in an effort to shake the ache, but nothing
I did worked. I traded eternal peace for short-lived
moments of ecstasy until I couldn't deny what I was
feeling even when I couldn't find the words for it.

I asked my therapist about it. "You're looking for
intimacy," she suggested. I didn't buy it. As an introvert, the last thing I needed was another friend. But
I started to notice the cracks in my life. I started to

see that despite how much I knew about God, I didn't really trust Him. Without the distraction of the hustle, I had plenty of time to be silent. I had plenty of time to think, to listen. I went on long walks where I would pray. Don't be that impressed. My prayers weren't Instagrammable. Sometimes all I could do was mumble. Other times, if I could muster the words, I prayed, "God ... are you there?" I looked for red cardinals because they felt like a divine epiphany. I didn't have energy for social media, which helped way more than I thought it could. I sat on my patio for hours at a time, listening, breathing, being. I started to notice that when everyone else was gone, God was still there.

Slowly it occurred to me that my therapist was right. I *was* looking for intimacy, but I didn't need a new friend to learn the language of intimacy. I just needed more time with my oldest one.

Did you know that trust is the language of intimacy? It takes silence and time and practice to learn it. It's a language that can only be learned in stillness, away from the hustle. Slowly but surely, I was learning to trust again.

We've adopted a Christian model in the church that doesn't work. We were created for intimacy with God that can only be learned in quiet and vulnerability. Instead, we've bought into the lie of busyness and hustle. We've accepted a model that has left us hungry for connection. In our rush to keep up the hustle, we've settled for any kind of false intimacy that leaves us desperate for something deeper, more real. The busier for Jesus we become, the lonelier we feel. Emotional isolation and sexual struggle go hand in hand like PB and J. Or like chips and guac. Once you take that first bite, it's hard to stop.

No wonder so many tired, exhausted hustlers turn to porn and affairs. It's a world that puts "me" at the center of it all, a world that demands so little of me and provides unlimited pleasure. It's a world that centers on my needs and my wants, a world where I am the hero.

Not all hustlers struggle sexually. I get that. Your struggle may be much more respectable. We all do whatever it takes to quiet the ache inside. We're all broken, lonely people in need of constant affirmation and love. It's why social media is still going strong with no sign of leaving. But it's the ache that awakens us to what we really need.

When our schedules are too busy, our souls become empty. And when our souls become empty enough, we turn to whatever it is that helps make it better. Maybe it's time to reverse that. What if we encouraged people to build lives that might look like failure in the eyes of the world but are successful for our souls? What if we taught people the truth—that hustle is the kryptonite for intimacy? What if pastors and leaders embraced and modeled the Jesus way instead?

"Come away by yourselves . . . and rest a while" (Mark 6:31). Jesus once invited anyone who would listen.

If only I'd listened.

"Come to me, all who labor and are heavy laden, and I will l give you rest" (Matthew 11:28). He invited His followers once again.

This time I would take Him up on it.

There once was a bifurcation in the road. I would have stayed on the path like everyone else in the world—hustle, release, repeat. Mercy shoved me onto the road less taken.

I'm finally learning to breathe.

# THE BIG LOVE

*You're still the one I run to....*
*You're still the one I want for life.*
—SHANIA TWAIN


*You—complete me.*
—JERRY MCGUIRE

I'VE ALWAYS DREAMED OF FINDING THE BIG LOVE. IT'S probably why I'm still single. I've been waiting for the kind of love that makes people do crazy things, like move across the country or give up their trust fund. The kind of love worth dying for and living for and that cannot be contained.

The idea of the big love is really, really sexy these days. The notion that there is a man or woman out there who was created just for you—your soulmate. Someone who will complete you. And finish your sentences for you. And understand your deepest thoughts just by looking at you.

The message in our Western culture is that everyone needs, even deserves, this kind of big love. This is the love that will unleash our true selves and make us unstoppable. Grown men have bought into it enough to justify their affairs. "You don't understand," he explains to his brokenhearted wife, "I've fallen so madly in love. I can't help myself. I have to keep seeing her or I'll die." We have created a world where this kind of love justifies all wrongs and is the highest good. We have changed our sexuality for this kind of love. We have justified disintegrating our families in order to pursue this big and unstoppable love.

I sat on the floor of a tent in a Syrian refugee camp recently. My hostess was a woman around forty-five although she looked sixty. Every so often someone popped into the main room of the tent to huddle around the heater. She told me her story. She told me that she had been married at fifteen. She'd had eight kids by the time she was twenty-eight, besides her three miscarriages. Her oldest three were now married—all of them in arranged marriages by the time they had turned sixteen. After fleeing Syria a few years ago, they had landed in Lebanon and settled in the very tent we were sipping tea in. They were used to it by now. I asked her how many people lived in this tent. She needed a minute to count—fifteen, she answered, plus or minus three. "How did you meet your husband?" I probed. She chuckled. "My parents set it up. I met him on our wedding day." I notice one of her daughters hiding a smile. "How old are you?" I ask. "Fifteen," she answers shyly. "Do you want to be married?" I press. "Actually, I'm engaged. To my second cousin," she informs me proudly. "Are you in love with him?" I can't help the question. She looks at me with a question in her eyes. She has no idea what I mean.

Here in America, we've been told the lie that unless we meet our big love, we will never be happy. And that when we do, it's worth losing everything for the sake of pursuing this love. But I'm looking at this beautiful Syrian refugee teenager and I wonder what to say.

How could I explain to a bride of fifteen stuck in a culture where she has no voice and no rights and no education and no money and no respect that unless she finds the big love she will never be happy? To her, a meal on the table each evening is happiness. A tent that doesn't leak is happiness.

I don't tell her about the big sexy Hollywood love that she will never meet.

Instead, I tell her about Jesus and the great big love He has for her.

There is a love that translates across the world. It's a love that refuses to break families apart. A love that frees. A love that heals. A love that sees. A love that stays.

When I finish, I notice that she has tears in her eyes.

She tells me that she's spent her whole life dreaming of finding a big love like this.

# GRACE

*Everybody wants to go to heaven,*
*but nobody wants to die.*
—ALBERT KING

SOMEWHERE IN MY FORTIES, TIRED AND WORN OUT OF trying to overcome my sexual struggle, I decided that grace would have to be enough for me. I figured that since I had been saved by grace, I would just have to live by grace. Which meant that I accepted that in this one area of my life, I might have a problem forever.

Christians are funny about grace. We love the concept of grace as long as it fits into our personal preferences and parameters. We love everything about grace, until we meet someone whom we don't feel deserves grace. We're mad about people who seem to take advantage of God and His grace. We divvy out grace based on what we deem is appropriate. But where does grace draw the line? How many times can one realistically pull the grace card?

Does a sex offender deserve grace? What if he was a onetime offender? How about the wife beater? But what if he was beating his wife only half the time he used to beat her? Is his improvement a sign of change? What about the pastor who steals from the offering plate? What about the husband who can't kick his porn habit? Or the gay cousin who says he is a Christian and still shows up to Christmas dinner with his boyfriend? When does grace say, "Enough already. You've gone too far"?

I can hear your arguments and I get it. These examples are not about grace. They're about consequences, and standing up for what's right, and protecting the abused, and refusing to turn a blind eye on sin. I totally get it. I grew up in it. I've been washed with the blood of fundamentalist doctrine and it's hard to shake, even after all these years. But I also believe that when it comes to grace, we talk a big talk in the Christian world. We just have a hard time applying it consistently.

I'm one to talk. I'm the biggest culprit of them all. And when it comes to dishing up grace, it's me I can't stand giving it to. I dose out grace to myself one tiny dropperful at a time, but who's keeping track?

I have one loud voice in my head. It's a voice that reminds me that sooner or later my sin will find me out, just you wait and see. I've spent an entire lifetime looking over my shoulder, wondering who would be the one to find me. I've kept waiting, even hoping, someone would find me. The burden of my sin has been too heavy to carry at times. I think about the relief it would be to finally be found out. I long for the freedom of living openly, honestly. Grace seems too easy a solution. I want absolution, I want to get what I deserve. Instead, I've been given grace—the grace of time, the grace of God's quiet beckoning presence waiting. I've never confused His silence with His approval. I've been waiting for His punishment, ready for it, like a kid in a Catholic school waiting for that paddle to drop. It's what I deserve.

Instead, God has given me His grace. Tired and worn out, I've run out of reasons to refuse it.

When it comes to sex, most of us know exactly what the Bible teaches. We know what's right and what's wrong. It's hardly ever been an issue of knowledge. It's the doing that's our problem. And the wanting. And the inability to stop wanting. Who needs another book reiterating the chapter and verse that tells us where we've sinned? We've already got that list down. We've memorized it. If only God would remove the wanting. Instead, in the crucible of our desperate wanting, He hands over His grace.

It seems too costly a gift to flippantly receive. So we resist it for a while, until we can't anymore.

A lot has been written about cheap grace. Bonhoeffer coined the term and it's stuck. Cheap grace is about grabbing all that Jesus offers us without the willingness of changing. I'm sure there are plenty of people sitting in their dark basements browsing the web or hiding in hotel rooms in clandestine affairs claiming to be Christian while enjoying the pleasures of sin for the moment, counting on God's grace to forgive them while they keep on doing whatever it is they're doing. They figure God already knew what He was getting into when He chose them. Some call that cheap grace. I call it self-deception.

But what about when you want to change and can't? Does God's grace apply here? Or does it depend on the magnitude of your sin? Does it depend on how many times you try to change? When do you stop being worthy of receiving God's grace?

I am not a theologian. I'm not even trying to be one. I'm an ER doctor and I work with a lot of people all of the time. Life is hard for us humans. Everything is more complicated than it should be. Some of us overeat to cope with our struggles. Others of us drink alcohol. Still others have leaned into marijuana. Or sex. Anything to numb the pain of life. I hurt when I hear the stories of my patients. I want to fix them all.

But not everyone wants to be fixed. Let me try to explain. Suppose I was seeing four patients who were all smokers:

The first one, John, tells me that smoking is actually not that bad for one's health and he has no interest in stopping. He believes I'm judgmental and hateful when I ask him to stop. The second patient, Ruby, tells me that she agrees that smoking is bad for her health, but she is not ready to stop. The third patient, Molly, knows smoking is bad for her health and that she would like to try and stop. She needs my help. The fourth patient, Trevon, can't look me in the eye when he tells me that he agrees that smoking is bad, has already tried to stop on a number of occasions—unsuccessfully—but would like to try again.

Which one of my patients is the easiest for you to judge? Which one of them elicits the most compassion? Who needs grace the most? Who seems to be the most reticent to receive it? Here's my take: John is a jerk, Ruby needs time, Molly is on the right path, but it's Trevon that I want to help the most. It's Trevon that breaks my heart. I'll do anything to help him stop smoking, no matter how long it takes me.

There is one other kind of patient I run into. Bob is the most difficult for me to treat. He's the guy who knows that smoking is wrong, wants to keep smoking anyway, blames me when he gets cancer, and still assumes that I'll treat him when his habit finally catches up with him. Bob makes me crazy, but I'll still be there for him when he needs my help. I can't help it. It's who I am, plus I've made a vow to heal those who need it.

Peter asked Jesus once how many times he was expected to forgive his brother or sister. Trying to be generous, Peter said, "Up to seven times?" Jesus wasn't impressed. Instead, He set the bar higher: "I tell you, not seven times, but seventy-seven times."

The point Jesus was making was that forgiveness never stops. Grace never stops.

As a recovering hustler and as someone who grew up in a Christian legalistic culture heavy on personal effort, grace is like a drink of cold water on a hot desert day. Grace is a gift you didn't expect to receive and can't believe you have. Grace is undeserved and can even feel self-indulgent. It's a lot easier for me to process hard work than to accept free grace. It's easy for us to swing the pendulum from one side to the other. We tend to mentally divide Christians into a grace camp or a truth camp. We disdain the other side. We call each other names. We avoid one another. We assume heaven will separate us eventually and that somehow God's vision for grace is more like what we think it is.

But what if it isn't? What if grace is more than an excuse for me to keep doing what I know I shouldn't be doing but also an invitation for me to grow in the ways I know I should be growing? It's God's grace, after all, that saves me. Christ did all the work for me. It's by grace I've been saved through faith; it is a work of God.[25] It's by God's grace that I did the receiving. It's also God's grace that grows me and changes me. It's God's grace that invites me to long for more of Jesus every day of my life. It's why I'm writing this book—as grace is changing me, I am able to process why I have struggled in the way that I have and have longed to change even more. But the book hasn't written itself. On most days, even when I don't feel like it, I open up my laptop and push myself into this place where thoughts turn into words turn into story turn into life. It's grace that wills me here. It's grace that keeps me here. It's grace that gives me life but also sustains me and helps me thrive. But first I have to show up. It's the showing up that's the hardest. Will I respond by faith to God's grace that is waiting to change me, or will I continue to wallow in my own pain?

It feels obscene for me to ask for grace when I don't deserve it. It feels lazy for me to ask for grace when I'm too tired to do my part in changing. It feels useless for me to ask for grace when my faith feels too weak to sustain me. It feels like I'm using God when all I want from Him is to absolve me of any wrongdoing. I have done my share of wallowing, but by God's grace, and His unbelievable mercy, He has lovingly continued to pursue me and help me get out of my self-imposed pit of punishment and self-pity.

As a recovering hustler and former legalist, I'm learning to be anchored by grace that gives me more than I deserve but invites me to be more than I can imagine.

There are a lot of things I don't understand about grace. I don't understand how grace applies to child molesters and rapists. I don't understand how grace applies to someone who beats his wife once a week now instead of five times a week. I don't understand why a person who cheats on his wife and walks out on his kids should have the same amount of grace as a single guy who can't stop masturbating. I don't understand why at times God gives us a lifetime of grace to try to change, but at other times, He brings us to a sudden halt with a severe punishment in order to stop us.

All I know about grace is that I need it desperately in my life.

The rest is background noise.

# CHANGE

*I know that there is pain, but you*
*Hold On for one more day, and ya*
*Break free from the chains.*
—WILSON PHILLIPS

DOES CHANGE HAPPEN SUDDENLY OR DOES IT HAPPEN slowly over time? Maybe it's a little bit of both.

A week after Kathleen started coming to my church, her house burned down. She called me in tears, not sure what to do. While I rallied the troops to help Kathleen, she did the most obvious next thing: she worked on moving to a new place. Whether she liked it or not, it was time for her to make a big change.

A good rule for life is this: if your house is burning down, it's time to do something! The smoke billowing from the windows is your sure sign to change. Here are some hints that your house is burning down, spiritually speaking: if you're hurting others with your sexual sin, if what you're doing is illegal, if you've been caught with your hand in the cookie jar and are still lying about it.

Most of the time when it comes to our sexual struggles as Christians, it's more like a slow carbon monoxide leak. Things might look all right from the outside, but they're not. We're being poisoned to death without even knowing it. By the time we start showing signs of illness, it's too late. If you want to avoid crashing the train, or burning the house down, now is the time to make a change. Waiting until your house burns down is plain stupid, and I know you're not stupid.

When it comes to sex, most of us can be a little bit stupid. Even though we know that our sexual struggle is hurting us, we can't imagine life without it. We resist changing. We forget that change *is* the Christian life, but it can be a lot harder than it sounds.

A few months after starting my medical work with Syrian refugees, I met a kindhearted young man named Hakeem who worked at the community center where we held our clinic. He invited me to his tent after clinic one afternoon, and because we were ahead of schedule, I went. I met his mother and the rest of his family. It was a beautiful spring day in the Beqaa' Valley in Lebanon. We sat outside drinking coffee while I heard more of his family's story.

They told me how hard it was when they first arrived from Syria to Lebanon. They were one of the lucky ones to find a tent to live in. They had applied for a visa to go to the West, as most Syrian refugees had done, and they were still waiting to hear from the United Nations.

A few months passed and I went back to Lebanon for another medical clinic. I was thrilled to see Hakeem again, now a couple of inches taller. "How's it going?" I asked him as we high-fived. He gave me a quick update on the family. "How's your visa status coming along?" I wondered. His answer was slow to come, and when it did, I was baffled: "Well ... we got the visa, but we decided not to go."

Hakeem's family is not the only Syrian refugee family who has had a similar experience. No matter how difficult our present circumstances are, the mess we're in is often more comfortable than the unknown out there.

Change is hard no matter what shape or size it comes in. It's easier to hang on to the status quo. What makes change even harder are the times when we try to change and fail. It's demoralizing. It's defeating. It's confusing and it feels like a waste of time. What's the point of trying to change if we're going to end up exactly like we started?

If change were easy, people would be doing it all the time. Obese people would just stop overeating. Smokers would burn their cigarettes. Drug addicts would dump their bongs. And lazy people would actually use their gym memberships. Even jobs are hard to change. The only thing we seem readily willing to change these days are our spouses, our outfits, and our gender.

But change is not an option for the Christian stuck in sexual sin. It's survival.

Back in my twenties, I had all kinds of strategies for change. I tried praying about it. I tried fasting through it. I once heard that if you did something for twenty-one days it became a habit, so I did that for a while. No matter what I tried, given enough time and enough frustration in my life, I found myself back in the same pattern of numbing my pain with what felt good for a season. I was stuck.

I convinced myself that change was impossible for me. I simply couldn't change who I was. I was a sexual being for better or for worse. I simply couldn't change the essence of who I was created to be.

Then I met Laura. We were both guest speakers at the same conference. She was a kindhearted, gentle woman about five feet two in height. She started telling her story from the stage and I was riveted. She told us about how she had grown up in a Christian home. After leaving home, she started struggling with her sexuality and, later, her identity. She became so convinced that she identified as a man that she went through hormonal therapy. She was weeks before her transition surgery when she had an encounter with God and eventually gave her life to Jesus and transitioned back to her original God-given sexual identity.[26]

I guess change is possible for some people.

Christians are too binary when it comes to change. We think that change should be very black and white. We're either changed or unchanged. We use Scripture to support our thesis: I once was blind and now I see. I've made the mistake of confusing the crisis that leads to new life with the process that leads to a transformed life. It's both crisis and process.

When a baby comes out of the birth canal, it's sudden and magical and ... well, actually it's gooey and sticky too. But you get the picture. It's dramatic to see the change that happens before the baby is born and after. As the baby grows, change happens in seasons. In some seasons of life, a growth spurt can be dramatic. In other seasons of life, it takes your great-aunt Mabel showing up to Thanksgiving dinner to remind you just how tall you're becoming, or how much you've changed.

Change isn't always straightforward. It's a process, and sometimes, a bumpy process.

My nephews are college athletes. They play football at a D1 school. In other words, they're serious about change. I look at their pictures from two years ago and can't believe how much they've changed. They're bigger and taller and stronger than they used to be. It's been a slow process that has taken time and effort. They watch what they eat. They watch when they sleep. They hit the gym every single day except the days they take off. It's exhausting just listening to them. Most of us wouldn't dream of living the way they live.

When Micah was a sophomore, one of his teammates tore his ACL. He had to have surgery and was sidelined for a while. In time, he started training again, and after several months of agonizing pain and work, he played again. His other friend was benched for a while until he put on enough weight to get back on the line. Still another one's grades were suffering so he had to step down from playing for a season. Just because those guys weren't on the front line didn't make them any less a part of the team. Each problem they faced brought about the need to change, and change took time and patience. It was a process.

Change is a bit more fluid than I want it to be. Each time I've tried to change, I've done okay for a while—until I slipped back into old habits. When I fail and find myself struggling again, I judge myself too harshly, calling myself a hypocrite. I conclude that at the very least, God must be very disappointed in me.

But what if the times when I've slipped back into old habits were the equivalent of a football injury? What if instead of assuming my failures are final, I start to accept them as part of the process and do the work needed to get back into shape?

Change happens in increments, slowly over time. God still loves us when we hit the road bumps.

My friend Suzie is even more cynical than I am. She tells me that people can't change. That at the end of the day, we are who we are. I don't agree. I believe anyone can change. You just have to figure out the why. It's the why that matters. If you know why you need to change, the rest is doable. If you don't have a why, you're screwed.

Do you know your why? It's taken me a minute to figure out my why. And sometimes I'm prone to forget.

When my nephew Sam was little, he would come over to my house to hang out. He loved helping me with jobs around the house. He still likes to help me. Honestly? I don't need his help 99 percent of the time. It takes me four times longer to get something done when he helps. But it's the process of doing it together that has deepened our relationship. We are closer today because I've been there for him when he needed my help to get things done.

God, being God, could change me in a heartbeat. But He hasn't. Instead, He invites me into the process of leaning on Him and needing Him in my most challenging places. I hate that I can't do this on my own. I hate that I still want what I know I shouldn't want. It's tempting to want to rewrite my story without those seasons in my life when I've been most tempted to struggle sexually. But I'm starting to see that those seasons are God's invitation for me to lean on Him even more. It's about deepening our relationship. It's about love.

We humans value the outcome of change: success. God loves the process of change: dependence.

I usually have one goal when I think about changing my habits: to win. To overcome. To get over the problem. Sometimes it's even holiness I'm after. But holiness as an end point is still not the point. Underneath this desire to win is my mistaken belief that if I could just win in this area of my life, God will finally reward me. He'll make all my dreams come true.

I've made the subtle mistake of using Jesus to achieve my holiness—hoping that if I'm holy enough God will be pleased enough with me to do whatever it is I want Him to do for me. What God offers me is Jesus, with holiness as a natural but secondary outcome.

Real change happens when we stop worrying about the outcome and start focusing on Jesus.

As hard as it is to change, people *do* change all the time. My Peloton instructors preach change day in and day out. Their stories are testimony that our behaviors as humans can change. They tell me I'm strong enough to achieve anything I put my mind to. Yet all over the world are people who claim to follow Jesus who are still just as mean and just as addicted and just as angry and just as fearful as everyone else. Why does it sometimes seem even harder for followers of Jesus to change than the rest of the world?

What God wants for us isn't just behavior modification, but heart transformation. The reason this kind of change is harder is that it doesn't demand as much action from us. Action is heroic, and when change depends on me being the hero, move over world. But God's version of change is a different kind of radical. All it requires is a whole lot of yielding. Jesus asks us to give Him everything: our values, our wants, our dreams, our sexuality, our future—yes, even our whole lives! It's a total takeover!

He knew it wouldn't be easy. It's why He warned us to count the cost before jumping in. It's why He said that the road leading to Him is so narrow. It's why He reminded us to carry our cross and deny ourselves every single day. Like brushing our teeth or wearing clothes. Some things can't be negotiable.

When it comes to my sexual struggle, I want magic. I want an apostle Paul kind of transformation. I want a testimony where one day I'm struggling with sexual sin, and the next day I'm free. I've judged anything less than that as failure. But change for me has been a slower process, a daily process. It's one step forward and two steps back. It's celebrating the wins and quickly confessing where I've failed. Where I have wanted magic, God has given me persistent need. Need has been my Achilles' heel, but it's also been my place of grace. Need has served at times as an excuse for me to yield to the struggle, but it is always an invitation for me to depend on Jesus and His unconditional love for me.

Life is meant to be lived one day at a time. Every day I'm given a choice.

Will it be Jesus or me?

Don't wait until your house is burning down. Stop fooling yourself into thinking the carbon monoxide isn't going to kill you.

Today is a good day to change.

# FUTILE FORMULAS

*Eat, sleep and breathe it, rehearse and repeat it,*
*'cause I got new rules, I count 'em.*
—Dua Lipa

*Don't know much about history.*
*Don't know much biology....*
*But I do know that I love you.*
—Sam Cooke

WHEN I WAS IN MY LATE TWENTIES, I READ A BOOK about fasting that said if you fasted three days, God would finally answer your prayers. I wanted so badly to change. I wanted freedom from my sexual struggle. I started the fast but lasted only two days. I've often wondered ... what if that was the reason I kept failing?

Everyone loves a good formula.

I call my mom and ask her about a recipe she makes. No, wait, that isn't me. I don't cook. It's my niece who calls and asks for a recipe. My mom lists the ingredients and tells her to put a little of this and a little of that and ta-da! My niece is not mollified. She wants to know exactly how much of each ingredient. How many teaspoons of sugar. How many dashes of salt. Where my mom sees in art, my niece sees in formulas.

Formulas make us feel like we've got it. We can't screw this up. We've got the list to prove it. When we don't get the desired outcome, we assume we got the wrong formula, so we go hunting for another formula. We do that for a while.

I tried content-restricting software on my phone. Of course I did. What do you think I am, a heathen?

I thought it would solve all my problems. But then I had a patient with herpes. I needed to check the dose of the medication, but I was blocked by the software. My problems were with Amazon anyway, so I tried blocking Amazon, but ... I'm a single girl living in the twenty-first century. Living without Amazon Prime was like living without oxygen. Content-restricting software wasn't for me.

For a while I used the built-in content restrictions on my iPhone. The only problem with that formula was that I always knew the password since I had set it up! I talked my sister once into putting a password in so I wouldn't break the code. I felt it was more honorable that way. A few weeks later, I needed the password for some reason or another, but my memory-challenged sister had forgotten it. I had to get a new iPhone to resolve that hiccup because even the Genius Bar couldn't break the code my sister had created.

Christians love formulas. We have formulas for our quiet time. We have formulas for our church services. We have formulas for our Bible study guides. We have formulas for our sermons. We have formulas for child rearing and parenting and marriage and dating. We have formulas for friendships and Enneagrams; we have formulas for eating and drinking. If you've ever wondered about it, Christians have a formula for it that they'll sell you in a book with a stack of additional resources to help you remember them.

We've even turned repentance into a formula. You can confess your sin to God, but it doesn't count as much if you don't tell a live human being and set up an accountability plan. You can pray, but if you don't start with repentance, God won't hear your prayers. I've done that before. I've used repentance hoping to manipulate God to do what I want Him to do. I'll spare you the trouble of trying this formula; it doesn't work.

One of my nephews called me the other day. "I'm struggling to love people, Lina. Help me out. Everyone gets on my nerves all the time. I've prayed about it so much. I've even memorized 1 Corinthians 13." I chuckled. He inherited my gene when it comes to his personality. Even the love chapter wasn't doing it for my poor nephew. I wasn't surprised. Been there, done that.

The try harder formula is the most popular formula for Christians to use. We love our efforts. We journal. We memorize. We pray. We walk on coals. We stand outside in negative 30-degree weather. We go to church and stay later than everyone else. We go to midweek church. We join a small group. When we start to feel like one isn't enough, we join a second.

No matter how hard we work, eventually the work formula fails us. It's because we weren't wired to work our way to perfection. We're wired for more. We're wired for freedom.

When I turned forty, I weighed myself and calculated that if I continued the trajectory I was on with gaining weight, I would be over four hundred pounds by the time I retired. I got nervous enough to make a drastic change. I decided to go keto. I gave up the one food group that had sustained me most of my life: carbs. It sounded impossible. I didn't think I could do it. I went live on Facebook and told everyone and cleaned out my fridge right there. Because, you know, if you do something live on social media, it's more real. There was nothing left in the fridge by the time I was done. People cheered me on. I felt like Rocky on the stairs of the Philadelphia Museum of Art. It was inspiring. I was a martyr and willing to bear that burden for the glory that was to come.

I lost twenty pounds. I looked good for a while. The keto diet lasted six months. Then little by little, a bread slice here, a dinner roll there, and I was back in my sweet spot (see what I did there?).

The sacrifice formula is hard, and it works for a little while until it doesn't. It's because it demands willpower. Willpower starts out strong but eventually fizzles out. Once my weight dropped a little, it was harder for me to justify sacrificing carbs.

What was one cookie going to harm anyway? But one cookie led to two, and eventually, it just didn't matter as much anymore. I've done the same with my sex problem. I've sacrificed Netflix for a while, restricted the Internet, but after a week, a month, a season, I hear everyone talking about a cool new show. I reinstall Netflix. Next thing I know, I'm back to square one.

Even accountability has turned into a formula. Christian leaders talk about the merits of accountability to ward off sexual sin. All over the United States are churches full of small groups, men's groups in particular, where sin is confessed almost ritualistically week after week but where change remains elusive.

Formulas—even the good ones—don't work, and when they do work, they take us only so far. The problem with formulas is that they are often void of the Holy Spirit. They put the burden of change on me, instead of on God. But the process of transformation for the Christian is a God-driven process. The harder I've tried to change on my own, the more frustrated I've become.

I have spent days and weeks doubting God's love for me because of my own failed formulas. Why wasn't I changing despite doing what He wanted me to do? Was I even a Christian since the formulas weren't working for me?

But what if I was going about it all wrong? What if my main problem was that I was still trying to live the Christian life without Jesus?

For too long I've made the end point of my formulas to be victory over my sexual struggle. In some way, I suppose I've tried to use Jesus to help me get over this blemish on my record. I've wanted to be perfect in every way possible. I want everyone to know that I've got it together. I think my motives have been decent. I've assumed that if people see how good I am, they'll admire this Jesus who has helped me be this way.

There's only one problem with my theory: Jesus didn't ask me to be perfect. He just asked me to be His.

There was a rich young man who came to see Jesus once. He knew the formulas really well. You could say he was an expert in the formulas. He had memorized the formulas. He had everything going for him, and everyone thought so too. He asked Jesus what mattered the most in life. Maybe he was curious about the answer or maybe he just wanted to make the point that he already had the right formulas. I can't answer that. But Jesus's response is what matters. Jesus didn't care as much about the formulas. What Jesus cared most about was the man's heart. Jesus wanted his heart. In other words, Jesus wanted everything.[27]

It's not perfection or admiration or formulas Jesus wants. It's our hearts. It's our worship.

When worshipping Jesus becomes the focus of our lives, formulas become irrelevant, and change is inevitable.

# ECSTASY

*I can't get no satisfaction.*
*'Cause I try, and I try, and I try, and I try.*
—THE ROLLING STONES

BACK IN THE DAYS WHEN I USED TO BLOG, I WROTE AN article that I titled "Will There Be Sex in Heaven?" The premise of the article was that for single celibate people like me, the idea that heaven will be a place where sex is absent is disappointing, to say the least. But being the good Christian that I am, I concluded by what is often taught in churches—that we won't even be thinking about sex in heaven because we'll be with God, and He is much more delightful. Than sex.

Okay, now, if you're a boomer and you just had to convince your spouse to get it on last night, I can see why you're looking forward to a heaven without sex, but can you understand why that kind of logic is grating to single people like me? You guys get to have the cake and eat it, while we … don't.

Don't get me wrong, I do believe God is delightful. But technically, God is with me now. Shouldn't I already be experiencing Him as delightful? Shouldn't God-related activities already be satisfying me? So why does the idea of watching reruns of *Seinfeld* on any given night sound more entertaining for most of us than praying for missionaries around the world?

I believe churches have done a horrible job of teaching us how to enjoy God. Everything we've been taught about God and our walk with God is so full of "shoulds." We should be reading our Bibles every day. We should be memorizing Scripture. We should be in a small group. We should be confessing our sins to one another. We should be tithing. We should be kind to our neighbors. We shouldn't watch this. We should go there. It's exhausting. It's duty, duty, duty. No wonder leaders fail. Maybe they're tired of all the shoulds. Maybe they can't keep up the facade. No one can. But I'm not even sure that's what Jesus had in mind for us when He invited us to follow Him.

When I think about Jesus's time on earth, I see a completely different model. One of the most striking pictures of the Christian walk is early in the ministry life of Jesus. He was walking by the Sea of Galilee when he saw two brothers, Simon Peter and Andrew. He invites them to follow Him. They are so compelled by this man that they literally bail on the family business, leave the only job they knew well, their whole livelihood in fact, and actually follow Him. Can you even imagine the conversation they had with their father that day?

When Peter and Andrew left everything to follow Jesus, they weren't dreaming of a life of sitting at their desk by candlelight memorizing the Torah.

They weren't leaving everything to spend their days writing down three points about God they gleaned from the Ten Commandments. No! They wanted action and adventure. They wanted something they'd only ever dreamed of. They wanted to see change and breakthrough and love in action. They longed for more. They wanted a life full of ecstasy. And they got it. Life turned upside down for them that day.

There are two other pictures of the effect of Jesus on His followers in the Gospels. The first is when Jesus was crucified. When the road got hard, the disciples, the very same ones who had given up everything to follow Jesus, scattered in disappointment. How could Jesus let them down like that? They were hurt. They were confused. They were devastated. One by one, they went back to their own vices. Thomas to his doubt. Peter to his boat.

And then something happened that changed everything for those same disciples. The last encounter we see of Jesus on earth is after His resurrection. Here we see the same disciples who had initially been ecstatic about following Jesus, then later devastated by the outcome of their decision, now fully back on board with fire in their guts. Their eyes have been opened. All the things they had hoped for did take place but in a way that surpassed every one of their expectations. To say that life was never the same for them after the resurrection is an understatement. They eventually died for the sake of Jesus, this risen Savior. They never looked back. Not one of the eleven disciples (minus Judas) ever succumbed to sexual struggle. I'm not suggesting they didn't struggle, but that none of them were discounted for sexual failure. Rather, they did warn the early Christians about sex outside of God's parameters, but they seemed to wear Kevlar when it came to their own private lives. Their eyes were fixed on someone that had so captured their attention, it's hard for us to even imagine it.

In all my readings of the New Testament, never do I get the impression that the disciples sat around in a room hashing out what Jesus really meant when He told them to love their enemies. Never do we see them endlessly debate who the enemy really was. They didn't build factions about when adultery was permissible. They didn't fight about what retaliation really looked like. In all my readings of the New Testament, never do I see the disciples huddled in a room memorizing the Beatitudes and applauding one another for getting the order right. Never in all my readings of the New Testament do I see the disciples sleeping through a prayer meeting outside of the one in the garden of Gethsemane.

For the early disciples of Jesus, life in Christ was an adventure. It was fun. It was hard, yes, and dangerous, for sure, but it was exciting and ecstatic. It was a delight to be called a follower of Jesus even though it would eventually cost them their life.

What have we done to living the Christian life? When did we make it so duty driven, discipline focused, heavy and exhausting, and bent on do's and don'ts? Most Christians I meet look most like the disciples in the middle phase of life, during the post-crucifixion season of disappointment. To the watching world, we are a lot more like crucifixion people instead of resurrection people.

No wonder we've looked for the ecstasy of a short-term orgasm to fill our time. It's the closest to an adventure most Christians in the West will have these days. It seems to me that most Christians have a narrow view of who Jesus is and what He's up to. Our view of God is inaccurate. It's been shaped by a bunch of old fogies more comfortable with a rule book than with leading the family business into the unknown future.

I was tired of living my life under the weight of a bunch of shoulds with the promise that when I did eventually get to heaven, I'd finally get this Jesus, but without the fun of all things orgasmic. It seemed like a letdown.

*Orgasm.* It's funny to me that the word itself makes us cringe. "Orgasm" can technically be a medical term. It is a God-created concept. I'm sure there have been volumes written by theology professors and seminarians on the similarities between orgasms in marriage and the beauty and ecstasy of oneness in Christ. I haven't read them yet. But I have longed for a life in Christ here on earth that feels remotely like a life full of adventures and orgasms—and I don't mean that in the literal way.

I watched the revival at Asbury University unfold in the spring of 2023. One of the most memorable descriptions I heard from more than one student was the idea that time flew by. One student talked about how she went into chapel and thought she had been there for an hour, but eight hours had passed. She hadn't even checked her phone. No one checked their phones. The Spirit of God did something in the hearts of the people that was more important, more orgasmic, so to speak, than checking their Snapchats. If that isn't a movement of God, I'm not sure what is.

I can hardly sit through church anymore without checking my phone. I long for more—more excitement, more adventure, more resurrection power, more action, more feelings, more beauty, more life in Christ, than I've experienced in the American church.

No wonder we look for temporary orgasms any way we can get them. No wonder leaders crack and chase whatever temporary pleasure they can grasp. I'm not excusing their mistakes, their sins, their patterns. I'm just wondering if we've limited our view of God to our mundane lives to the point where anything that makes us feel something is a welcome consolation.

There have been a few times when I have felt something close to ecstasy in my walk with the Lord. My friend Deanna commented on this once. She was looking at a picture of me surrounded by Muslim women in Jordan right around when the refugee crisis was unfolding. She said, "You look alive when you're on a mission trip." I've been to Africa, to Lebanon, to Jordan, to China. Each time I'm out there serving God in the wild, I've felt alive. I can't remember ever struggling with my flesh in those seasons. Not even once.

Could it be that we've misunderstood what Jesus meant when He said, "Follow me, and I will make you fishers of men"? (Matthew 4:19) Could it be that we've settled for an American version of it that feels like shackles to our souls?

I missed Jesus. For me that was the biggest reason I finally came to my senses.

I had had glimpses of Him in my youth. I'd experienced His voice in my life asking me to follow Him, but it had been so long that I sensed this wild call to follow Him. Things had become so mundane. Church had become a prison of duty. Christian institutions in all their variety started to feel more and more like a performance trap where nothing was ever good enough. It didn't matter how many books I wrote, or how many tweets about Jesus I dropped, or how many conferences I spoke at—it was never enough. Everyone was always competing to see who would be the one to sit at the right hand of Jesus and at His left.

Have you ever felt like you're sleepwalking through life? Your head feels like it's in a fog. You know something feels off but you're not sure what. That's how I felt for a while. It was like watching myself from outside my body. I wanted to wake up. I needed to wake up.

I want my life with Jesus to be fun. I can already hear the cynics. We're not supposed to have fun with Jesus. We're supposed to be holy. God didn't create us to be happy, but to be holy. Do you think the disciples missed that memo after the resurrection? It seems to me that the opposite was true. The disciples on the road to Emmaus couldn't control their joy after their eyes were opened to the risen Jesus. Paul wrote his letter to the Philippians from a prison cell, and to this day, we call that letter the happy letter or the letter of joy, depending on how stodgy you think Christians should be.

The point is, the disciples loved living the Christian life. They didn't have time for fake orgasms.

Some people are good at fun. I'm not one of them. It doesn't matter how many books I read about fun, it's just not in my rolodex of skills. I have been wired and brought up to work. I study. I hustle. I focus. I'm intense, and it's exhausting. There are very few spaces in my life where I am given the freedom to let go. It's been destructive to my walk with Jesus.

I got tired of feeling bad about reading less than three chapters of the Bible in my daily time with God. I got tired of New Year's resolutions where I promised myself I'd memorize more Scripture this year, then failed. I got tired of living my life with Jesus where I couldn't wait to get through my Christian duties so I could finally really relax and watch some Netflix.

I long for a life where my time with Jesus is my time of ecstasy. I long for a life where I am not always waiting for the other shoe to drop. I long for a life where my Christian worth and impact isn't judged by how many followers I have. I long to be free— completely and unquestionably free.

We're living in the most depressed generation of all time. We're living in the loneliest generation of all time. I read an op-ed in the *New York Times* recently that said that we should be having more sex in our culture as a cure for loneliness.[28] That's how bad things have gotten.

We don't need more sex, but we do need more ecstasy. We need a life bigger than our own. We need our imaginations reignited again by the fire of the Holy Spirit. We need to move out of our small groups and into the big bad world out there, where instead of memorizing Bible verses, we're living them.

We don't need to stop being lovers of "pleasure" as if pleasure is a bad thing, but we do desperately need to redefine what pleasure really is. We need a church that demonstrates life more attractive than *Seinfeld* reruns. Can you even imagine the apostle Paul hanging out in his basement watching reruns of anything? He was too busy living his life for reruns.

Instead of resenting God for the monotonous lives we've created, perhaps it's time we accept His invitation to real life, to abundant life, to freedom. But in order to do that, we need to take our eyes off of the disappointment of the crucifixion and fix them on the joy of the resurrection.

I am in no way lessening the power of the crucifixion to eradicate my sin, but I am sick and tired of living my life stuck in the tomb, settling for whatever feels good here and now because of a limited view of the risen Christ.

It's time for all of us to experience the ecstasy of the resurrection.

I've missed that Jesus, the risen one, and I will never ever live without Him again.

# SAFE PEOPLE

*And I know I can tell you anything.*
*You won't judge.*
*You're just listening, yeah.*
*'Cause you're the best thing.*
*that ever happened*
*to me.*
—TOM WALKER

I PRACTICED THE CONVERSATION IN MY HEAD SO MANY times my brain started to hurt. I pictured myself sitting on the velvet recliner in my friend's living room, Bible in my lap, waiting for the Bible study to end. At that point, we would go around the room and each person would ask for prayer. Technically, this is when Christians take turns confessing stuff in our lives that we're struggling with. In my imagination, it would be my turn, and I would finally build up enough courage to say the words out loud: "I'm struggling with lust, and I can't stop masturbating."

But I couldn't do it. Week after week, I would freeze. The words out of my mouth were a little more like this: "Pray for me. I'm struggling with worry. I have a big exam next week. And also, pray for continued victory in my thought life." Everyone would nod their heads and jot down my name and prayer request. Then they'd move to the next lady in the room.

Fast-forward a couple of decades. As a jaded fifty-year-old virgin, I'm tempted to roll my eyes and smirk. Why was it so hard to say the obvious? Yet in my ten years or more of going to small group regularly, I have never had a woman in my small group

ever say anything about a porn addiction or masturbating, or having an affair, or thinking about having
an affair. Not once.

Given the stats, it's hard to believe: Ninety-
four percent of kids will see porn by age fourteen.
Seventy-six percent of Christian adults eighteen to
twenty-four years old actively search for porn. Thirty-
three percent of women under twenty-five search
for porn at least once per month. Only 13 percent
of self-identified Christian women say they never
watch porn. Twenty-five percent of married women
say they watch porn at least once a month.[29] And one
in six (17 percent) married women are cheating on
their spouses. That's better than the men, where one
in three (35 percent) married men are having sexual
affairs.[30] That means that if my small group has six
women in it, one is cheating and a few are checking
out porn once a month. Who knew?

The truth is that I didn't feel safe telling anyone
about my sexual struggle.

I racked my brain trying to think of a way to
casually drop the information into a conversation.
No matter what angle I considered, I couldn't realistically paint a narrative where I felt safe telling my
church people about my lust problem. Masturbating
and porn and affairs were forbidden topics for
women in my church world. I've heard that with men
the opposite is true. Everyone confesses to porn in

the men's small group. It's their thing. If you don't confess to porn, they think something is wrong with you. Then you show up again the following week and do it again. I wouldn't call that a safe practice, would you?

One day I decided enough was enough. I'd been in that particular small group for two years, and I felt good about the friends I'd made. So I planned it out. I would take the leader out to breakfast and make small talk for a while. Then, as I swallowed my last piece of bacon, I would tell her everything. My heart rate went up, my face turned beet red, I could barely breathe, but I was committed to the agenda. "The thing is," I mumbled, "the thing is, I struggle with masturbation and I'm sick of living a lie."

I don't remember the rest of the conversation, only that I was absolved of my guilt and that the topic was never brought up again. In hindsight, maybe she thought I said "maturation." Meanwhile, I still masturbated and wondered whether I was the only Christian in the world without a safe place to help me out of my mess.

My experience in medicine has been the very opposite. Just the other day I took a call from a patient who had noticed a weird vaginal discharge. She told me that the problem started after she had sexual intercourse with her partner. The partner noted the same thing on his penis. We talked for a few minutes while I tried to figure out the problem. She interrupted me and said, "Oh, I forgot to mention. What I meant by penis is really a dildo. My partner is a trans male. We do our best to clean the dildo, but I'm worried we didn't clean it well enough this time." Without batting an eye, I proceed to reassure her that no matter where the infection came from, we would treat her and she would survive to have yet another enjoyable sexual encounter.

Those weren't my exact words, but you get the gist. We were in a no-judgment zone and the patient knew it. She felt safe with me.

We tell our doctors and our therapists a whole lot of things that we don't tell other people because our doctors and therapists are safe. We know that they have our backs no matter what. We expect a certain level of compassion even if they don't agree with our decisions. We know that the moment we walk into that room, we are in a no-judgment zone.

Why can't Christians practice the same kind of compassion and acceptance to one another? Creating a safe space for the truth does not nullify consequences of sinful choices nor does it assume agreement. Creating a safe space means simply making space for people to tell the truth about their lives and to be met with compassion. It's a way to help people get the help they're not sure how to ask for.

If things were bad preCOVID, they've gotten worse since. We're living in the loneliest times of our lives. The CDC recently reported a record level of sadness and suicide risk among teen girls with a roughly 60 percent increase in sadness over the past decade. In 2021, 57 percent of high school girls reported experiencing persistent feelings of sadness or hopelessness in the past year, compared with 36 percent in 2011. Thirty-three percent reported they seriously considered attempting suicide in 2021, up from 19 percent in 2011.[31]

Don't be distracted by the stats. The story these statistics tell is simply that people are hurting. We're a lonely bunch. We're more depressed and anxious and hopeless than we've ever been before.

By the time a young person shows up to your church, they've already been exposed to porn for a while, they're likely experimenting sexually and not sure what they think about it, and they're feeling hopeless. If they do dare open up to someone about what they're going through, it's up for grabs whether the pastor of that church has a history of sexual abuse and will further prey on those young people or not. If you think I'm exaggerating, you haven't been paying attention to the sex abuse scandals in the Catholic Church or in the Southern Baptist churches. I'm not pointing fingers; I'm just stating facts.

These days, churches are the last place anyone will go to find a safe person to talk to.

I found my safe place in therapy. I found a judgment-free zone where I could confess my deepest fears and express my greatest worries knowing that I would find compassion. It was still paralyzing to get the words out of my mouth. I couldn't say the *M* word without stuttering. My therapist listened to me stumble through my confession. When I finally looked up, it felt like someone had let some light into the attic space I had kept shut for so long. There were cobwebs and there was a lot of dust, but little by little, we worked on cleaning things up. It was like a Joanna Gaines special. The musty attic was transformed into a welcoming extra loft bedroom.

Remember that time Jesus went to a well in the middle of the day? He ran into a woman known for her promiscuity. I've always had this mental picture that she was the dangerous one in the story, but any woman knows how threatening it can feel to be alone somewhere and have a man show up and start a conversation with you. I would have run the other way. Yet there must have been something about Jesus that felt safe. Well, Jesus didn't waste any time. He started a conversation with the woman and soon asked her some uncomfortable questions about her sexuality. He then helped her see the truth beneath her shame. When she could barely lift her head in shame, He gently looked her in the eyes and told her the same thing he whispers to us today: I'm your safe space. You belong here.

I don't know if you've noticed, but the sexual revolution has come and gone. Even though the church isn't sure what to make of it, the reality is that people in churches are bombarded by sex. They talk about it in their high schools and colleges and in their workplaces. They watch movies about it and read books about it. There is very little shame around the topic of sex until we walk into the sanctuary. The church has become the only place where the truth has to stay hidden in the attic and where people are judged by their secret and not-so-secret sins.

It's time for the church to demystify the conversation about sex. We need to create an environment that doesn't threaten those who are desperate for healing. We're all dying to tell someone. Hidden in our hearts are deeply held secrets ready to break free.

When I started writing my story, I chose my friend Bonnie to get the first look at the manuscript. My sister and my best friend Tina were miffed why I let Bonnie read it first. I chuckled. "It's because Bonnie's just as broken as I am. I can't shock or disappoint her." Bonnie was my safe place. She offered me a judgment-free zone.

The first people we will invite into our story are always the ones that we sense are just as broken as we are. The last ones we tell are the ones who admit to nothing. They've got the Christian life down. We can feel their disdain all the way across the room, and if we can't feel it, they'll remind us how disappointed they are in us with a sneer.

I like watching the end of marathons. There's always that guy. You wonder why he's even running, but there he is, limping, barely making it. A year ago, I saw a deeply inspiring video of a high school race where one guy was leading when his teammate who was a few steps behind him did something to his leg. Just short of the finish line, he went down. Instead of going for it, the guy who was leading turned back, helped his buddy up, and helped him limp his way to the finish line. They didn't win the race that day, but they won in life.

People don't set us free. Only Jesus does. Confession doesn't absolve us of our sin. Only Christ's death on the cross does. But people are who God uses to show us His love. That's how He rolls. He feels so strongly about it that He became a man to show us His love.

We create safe places for others when we tell our stories. That's very powerful. So tell your story. Tell it all. Tell the good, the bad, and the ugly. Tell it to your friends. Tell it to those who look like they're hurting. Tell it until it doesn't feel so awkward anymore. Tell it until you can say it without stuttering. Tell it until it stops hurting to hear the agonizing details of it all. Tell it until it becomes part of your past that has shaped you and formed you into the compassionate person you are today. Tell it until God starts to use it to build bridges to those who are desperate and hurting and longing to find rest.

And in your healing, watch God heal others around you with His rest.

Will we continue to beat each other up with the truth?

Or will we find Jesus in the church?

# PROMISES, PROMISES

*What if I stumble?*
*What if I fall?*
*What if I lose my step and*
*I make fools of us all?*
—DC TALK

I'M SO FULL I'M ABOUT TO EXPLODE. IT'S THANKSGIVING evening, and I literally have to prop myself up in bed in order to sleep. I promise myself that if I make it through the night, I will never, ever eat another meal again. The next morning, I'm two sips into my coffee when I meander my way to the kitchen in search of breakfast.

The problem with promises is that they're only as strong as the person who's making them. And humans are not very strong.

The husband sits with his wife, tears streaming down both their faces as he promises never to cheat again—until the next time it happens. The politician stands ramrod behind a mic promising never to sext anyone again—until he gets reelected and does it again. The pastor gets fired for sexual abuse, then a year later resurfaces on social media telling everyone he's learned his lesson and will never do it again, until he gets hired at his next church and tragically does it again.

We are rightfully cynical about promises. People just don't keep their promises very well.

I've got enough grace for people until about the fifth time I hear an apology. Actually, those who know me would suggest I might run out of steam after three "I'm sorry's." I'm intrigued by women who put up with more. My friend whose husband kept looking at porn lasted years before she finally said enough. And even when she did say enough, she felt guilt ridden that maybe she'd given up too soon. She had not. It was time to leave.

There's a fine balance between grace and enablement. There is no one formula that applies to everyone. Life is complicated, and sometimes you don't have the luxury to walk out. There is also a lot of judgment when someone does finally leave. We Christians are especially good at judging each other.

We're constantly in need of grace, God's grace.

If I'm cynical about other people's promise making, don't get me started on mine. I am an expert when it comes to making promises I can't keep, especially the ones I have no intention of keeping. I do it all the time. I tell friends I promise I'll come to their party when in reality, I'll never even try. I'm an unashamed introvert with no signs of changing. I promise myself I'll do more weight training, eat fewer desserts, plank for a few minutes each day. Blah, blah, blah.

With each broken promise is the growing realization that I can't. Given enough time, I'm very likely going to break that promise. Hypocrisy is deeply rooted in who I am. I need an excavator to dig it out.

I made it through medical school on empty promises. I promised God that if He helped me get into medical school, I would finally change. When I got into medical school, I promised God if He helped me graduate, I would change. Then I tried applying the same strategy to my love life. That didn't work as well for me. I've muddled through the last decade willing myself to keep my promises to God. I've not been that good at keeping my end of the bargain.

Is it better to make a promise and not keep it or not to make any promises at all?

I'm not as confident with the answer as I used to be. On the one hand, I might never do anything if I don't at least try. On the other hand, I don't like the feeling that I'm lying to myself and to God. With each broken promise comes the hollow realization that God already knows it's a matter of time before I fail. I've wrestled with my motives each time I've started a journal entry with "I promise."

Am I promising to change because I want to avoid negative consequences?

Am I promising to change because I am tired of the fight?

Am I promising to change because I want to protect my reputation?

Or am I promising to change because I want Jesus more?

My motives are always a little bit of this and a little bit of that. I'm a lot more like King Saul and a lot less like King David that way. Saul repented of his sin because he wanted God's favor.[32] David repented because he wanted God.[33]

What if God already knows that we're always going to struggle to keep our promises? What if He already knows this about us and still chooses to love us anyway? What if knowing how hypocritical we will turn out to be, He still made the choice to take on a human body, then suffer to death on a tree? What if He did it precisely because He knew we couldn't ever keep our promises, but that He could and He would? And that in His keeping His promises, we would be set free? What if knowing we would be so easily tempted by temporary pleasures, He still couldn't stop Himself from loving us?

Would you call Him dumb? Needy? Codependent? Gullible?

Or would you worship at His feet?

It's taken me a while to accept that I can't keep my promises. Only God can keep His promises. Lately instead of focusing on the promises I make to God, I'm holding on to the promises God has made me:

I am loved unconditionally.

I am forgiven eternally.

I am called by name.

I am not in this alone.

I can do anything with Christ who gives me strength.

I already have all that I need in Christ.

I have a purpose for my life that nothing can change.

I have a future coming soon that will be free of sexual struggle.

I have a daily purity streak going right now. It's getting longer each day. Will I break it someday? I hope not. I just have to get to ten thousand. I'll be seventy-seven by then. If I break my promise then, I'll give myself some grace.

Am I relying on a formula that won't work? Perhaps I am. But as long as I know there is a better way for me to live, I'm going to try. As long as my reason to change is more important than the thing I'm holding on to, I'm willing to try anything.

So, I'll hang on to the Billy Graham rule if I must. I'll show up to small group and give confession another try. I'll go to therapy as long as I need to. I'll stop making excuses. I'll breathe more deeply. I'll slow down a lot more often. I'll find my purpose in life and go after it with abandon. I'll even write a book if I must. But above all, I'll promise to receive God's grace for me when I do break my promises.

Don't let your broken promises keep you from God's love for you and His purpose for your life. I used to tell myself I'm fighting for holiness, but even that seems too limited a goal. It's Jesus I want. It's Jesus I need.

Back when I was younger, I used to cry out to God with promises I couldn't keep.

These days, I'm getting used to simply crying out to God.

# HOPE

*I can see clearly now the rain is gone.*
*I can see all obstacles in my way....*
*It's gonna be a bright*
*Bright sunshiny day.*
—JIMMY CLIFF

ONE YEAR AGO, I WAS ON THE PHONE WITH MY THERA-pist and wondered whether it might be too late for me to change. "What if it is?" she challenged me. "What if this is all you'll ever be? What have you learned about God so far?"

"Well, I'm still here," I responded.

I'm still here. One of the greatest signs of God's grace in my life is that I'm still here. Broken and tattered and worn out, I'm like the little stuffed animal that my nephew Sam still secretly hides under his sheets. I'm not going anywhere. Neither is God's love for me.

The realization slams into me with relief.

As long as I have breath, it's never too late for me to change. But change is not a requirement for God's love. God loves me. Period.

I don't need to do yoga to believe it. I don't need to center myself and write it down ten times in my journal. As sure as the sun rose this morning, God's love is over me. Under me. In me. For me.

How can it be? How can it be that God, this holy God, this awesome, magnificent, marvelous God, knows me so well and still loves me so much?

Is there room in the church for the sexually broken who might never change? Or is change a requirement that proves salvation?

Being set free from sin can easily become a story about me. Look at me now! I once struggled sexually, but now I am pure. But the story has never been about us. The story has always been about Jesus and His unexplainable love for us. Do you wonder if there is hope for you to change? Does the sun rise in the morning? Do birds sing? Do the stars shine at night? Does the lion roar and do monkeys hang from trees?

I've heard it said that hope is the belief that change is possible. I disagree. Hope is more than the belief that change is possible. Hope is the assurance that God's love will never change. Hope is resting in that love no matter what.

It's His love that changes us.

It's His love that is changing me.

I wish I could tell you that I am well past my struggle with lust. I won't tell a lie. The struggle remains. It's a daily act of surrender. I wish I could tell you that I've found the strategy for you to be set free. That's as ridiculous as telling my patients that I've found the cure for the common cold.

What I can tell you and what I'm learning is that God's love is enough for me. It's His love that sets me free. It's His love that is changing me.

To the pastor who has just been caught cheating on his wife—God's love is enough for you.

To the single man who can't stop masturbating—God's love is enough for you.

To the woman who is struggling with her sexuality—God's love is enough for you.

To the one who has been abused sexually—God's love is enough for you.

To the Christian who has been disillusioned by your leaders—God's love is enough for you.

To the woman who has been raped—God's love is enough for you.

To the one who has been betrayed by their lover—God's love is enough for you.

To the one who knows you don't deserve God's love anymore—God's love is enough for you.

To me on any given day—God's love is enough for me.

The people of Israel, after being freed from slavery in Egypt, got tired of waiting on God. They made a gold idol and worshipped it. The result was disastrous. God was hurt by the people of Israel, and thousands died that day. Worse than the plague they experienced was what happened after. The people of Israel heard that God was going to send them to the promised land without Him.

There was no greater punishment for the people of Israel than the idea of living life without God. The people were grieved. They mourned. They refused to go on. Moses interceded on behalf of his people. And God listened.

There is a greater tragedy than the tragedy of living without sexual fulfillment—it's the tragedy of living without God. Human parts eventually sag and weaken. Trust me. I've literally seen it. But God's love for us only grows stronger with time.

I can't explain His love. I don't understand it. But I have opened my heart to receive it. It's His love that sustains me. It's His mercy that has kept me. It's His grace that surrounds me. It's His presence that heals me.

It's never too late to change, because it's never too late to receive God's love. We are all undeserving of God's love, but we are all given a choice daily: will we surrender to God's love, or will we insist on finding satisfaction in what will leave us empty?

It's a no-brainer for me.

I'd rather stick with Jesus.

# EPILOGUE

THIS BOOK IS MY STORY. IT'S NOT A BIBLE STUDY OR A book on sexual ethics. It's not a reiteration of what the Bible says about gender and sexuality and infidelity and fornication. It's not a self-help book. If I'm being honest, there's not a problem I've met that I haven't tried to fix, but I can't fix you. Even with my amazing skills as a physician, I can't change you. Only Jesus can.

And oh, how much He loves you.

I hope you know Jesus and that you're experiencing the life-transforming love He has for you. I hope that after reading my story, you feel less alone. I hope you move from knowing about Jesus to knowing Him with every deep secret in your heart. The thing about freedom is that once you experience it, you have nothing left to hide. You move from not wanting anyone to know you're reading a book like this to being comfortable standing on the rooftops and sharing your story with everyone. But first you have to be willing to share it with one person. If you have no one else to share your struggle with, I'm here. I've created an online page where you can share your story with me: www.drlinabook.com. While it's not the answer to all your problems, it's a safe place to start.

Jesus is the only reason I'm here today. He's the only reason I am unafraid to tell my story. I have nothing to lose because I have already gained everything I need in Christ. He is worth every second of the battle for holiness.

I've shared my story as honestly and openly as I can because it needed to be done. Have you looked at our churches lately? We have a problem. Each story of a pastor's implosion is a reminder of how poorly we're doing on the Christian sex talk. Things have to change.

There is a need for bluntness and a directness to our conversation on sensitive matters these days. There is a need for honesty and vulnerability in talking about all things sacred. There is a need to expose every dirty little secret and step into the light.

If you're a critic, go ahead: analyze me, mock me, minimize my testimony, twist my words, exclude me, make excuses for me. None of it will matter. I am already fully known, fully loved, and fully accepted. My name is Lina, and I have been set free.

# UNDESERVED

Is mercy still mercy
When I've done it again
When I've used my last chances
When I knew but still did?

Is grace still grace
When I deserve what I get
When I'm stubborn at best
When I've failed every test?

Is love still love
When I've slammed my heart shut
When I refuse to give in
When I'm right no matter what?

O let mercy be mercy
When I need it the most
When I'm down on my knees
And my face's in the dirt.

And let grace still be grace
When I deserve it the least
When I feel like a mess
And I've nowhere to go.

O let love still be love
When my heart feels like stone
When my will's just my own
And I find I'm alone.

*Lina AbuJamra*

# ACKNOWLEDGMENTS

THE REASON THIS BOOK EXISTS IS BECAUSE OF THE people listed here who make it possible for me to still breathe each day and smile while doing it.

Diana: You're the best sister anyone could ever hope for. Also, you're stuck with me forever.

Irina: You're the reason we keep this thing going. Your loyalty moves and astounds me.

Tina: For easing the load on my back and making me laugh out loud. It takes someone truly special to understand my humor some days.

Sam: You're the best thing that happened to our family. Don't you forget that.

Don: How did we get so lucky to get you? My favorite day was the day you left publishing to start your own agency. Thanks for always having my back.

Bonnie: No words can express the gift you've given me in loving me just the way I am.

Margo: Can I mention one person more in this book? I don't think so. I promise you're never going to get rid of me.

Joy: Without your prayer support, I'd be lost. We're doing pretty good for not meeting yet!

Sarah: You are so much more than my token gay friend. Thanks for listening to anything I say.

Rosaria: Your voice in my life is a gift. Thank you.

My family: Sorry for making you uncomfortable, and thanks for riding this one out with me.

Becky: Thanks for your honest insight and for making this book stronger.

Everyone at Forefront Books: Jonathan, Jennifer, Lauren, Landon. You're the Jerry Maguire of publishing houses. Thanks for thinking out of the box with me.

LWP board: Thanks for trusting me on this one.

LWP community: You have encouraged me endlessly with your emails and support all these years. Thanks for loving on me no matter what.

Jesus: When words fail me, thanks for reading my heart. You're all I ever wanted and more.

# NOTES

1   Daniel Silliman and Kate Shellnutt, "Ravi Zacharias Hid Hundreds of Pictures of Women, Abuse during Massages, and a Rape Allegation," *Christianity Today*, February 11, 2021, https://www.christianitytoday.com/news/2021/february/ravi-zacharias-rzim-investigation-sexual-abuse-sexting-rape.html.

2   Morgan Lee, "Here's How 770 Pastors Describe Their Struggle with Porn," *Christianity Today*, January 26, 2016, https://www.christianitytoday.com/news/2016/january/how-pastors-struggle-porn-phenomenon-josh-mcdowell-barna; html. "Porn in the Digital Age: New Research Reveals 10 Trends," Barna Group, April 6, 2016, https://www.barna.com/research/porn-in-the-digital-age-new-research-reveals-10-trends/; Mark Martin, "Alarming Epidemic: Porn the Greatest Threat to the Cause of Christ," Christian Broadcasting Network News, April 2016, https://www1.cbn.com/cbnnews/health/2016/april/alarming-epidemic-porn-the-greatest-threat-to-the-cause-of-christ.

3   For more on the sexual confusion that has infiltrated the church, especially influencing younger Christians, see David J. Ayers, *After the Revolution: Sex and the Single Evangelical* (Bellingham, WA: Lexham Press, 2022).

4   Martin, "Alarming Epidemic."

5   Genesis 2:7:
Then the LORD God formed the man of dust from the ground and breathed into his nostrils the breath of life, and the man became a living creature.
Genesis 2:20–23:
The man gave names to all livestock and to the birds of the heavens and to every beast of the field. But for Adam there was not found a helper fit for him. So the LORD God caused a deep sleep to fall upon the man, and while he slept took one of his ribs and closed up its place with flesh. And the rib that the LORD God had taken from the man he made into a woman and brought her to the man. Then the man said,

"This at last is bone of my bones
  and flesh of my flesh;
 she shall be called Woman,
  because she was taken out of Man."
 See also Genesis 1:27:
 So God created man in his own image,
  in the image of God he created him;
  male and female he created them.

6  *Merriam-Webster*, s.v. "lust (n.)," https://www.merriam-webster.com/
   dictionary/lust.

7  Johannes Louw and Eugene Nida, *Greek-English Lexicon of the New
   Testament Based on Semantic Domains* (New York: United Bible
   Societies, 1989), 88:271; "4202. porneia," Bible Hub, https://biblehub.
   com/greek/4202.htm; "πορνεία," Bill Mounce, https://www.bill-
   mounce.com/greek-dictionary/porneia.

8  *Merriam-Webster*, s.v. "pornography (n.)," https://www.merriam-
   webster.com/dictionary/pornography.

9  "Porn in the Digital Age".

10 Amazon Best Sellers of 2023, March 2023, https://www.amazon.
   com/gp/bestsellers/2023/books.

11 Alexandra Alter, "How Colleen Hoover Rose to Rule the Best-Seller
   List," *New York Times*, October 9, 2022, https://www.nytimes.com/
   2022/10/09/books/colleen-hoover.html?smid=nytcore-ios-share&re
   ferringSource=articleShare.

12 Jeremy Wiles, "15 Mind-Blowing Statistics about Pornography
   and the Church," *Mission Frontiers*, November 1, 2020, https://www.
   missionfrontiers.org/issue/article/15-mind-blowing-statistics-abo
   ut-pornography-and-the-church.

13 "Church Chat: Satan," *Saturday Night Live,* https://youtu.be/
   FuJpalsj9sQ.

14 Danae King and Julie Fulton, "'Scourge of Sexual Abuse': Southern
   Baptists List Names 12 Ohio Pastors," *The Columbus Dispatch*, July
   5, 2022, https://www.dispatch.com/story/news/local/2022/07/05/
   southern-baptist-sexual-abuse-list-names-12-ohio-pastors/
   7786305001/.

15 Michael Slepian, "The Most Common Secrets We Keep,"
   *Psychology Today*, June 3, 2022, https://www.psychologytoday.com/
   us/blog/the-secrets-we-keep/202206/the-most-common-secrets-
   we-keep.

16 "Cannibal and Serial Killer Jeffrey Dahmer Is Caught," *History
   Channel,* July 22, 1991, https://www.history.com/this-day-in-history/

cannibal-and-serial-killer-jeffrey-dahmer-is-caught.

17  2 Samuel 11.

18  Billy Graham, "What's the Billy Graham Rule?" July 23, 2019, https://
    billygraham.org/story/the-modesto-manifesto-a-declaration-of-
    biblical-integrity/.

19  Albert Mohler, "The Tragedy of Joshua Harris: Sobering Thoughts
    for Evangelicals," August 1, 2019, https://albertmohler.com/2019/08/
    01/joshua-harris.

20  *Online Etymology Dictionary*, s.v. "masturbation (n.)," https://www.
    etymonline.com/word/masturbation.

21  Michele L. Yang, et. al., "Masturbation in Infancy and Early
    Childhood Presenting as a Movement Disorder: 12 Cases and a
    Review of the Literature," *Pediatrics* 116, no. 6(2005): 1427–32, https://
    publications.aap.org/pediatrics/article-abstract/116/6/1427/63005/
    Masturbation-in-Infancy-and-Early-Childhood?redirectedFrom=f
    ulltext.

22  John Piper, "Missions and Masturbation," *Desiring God*, September
    10, 1984, https://www.desiringgod.org/articles/missions-and-
    masturbation.

23  John Piper, "How to Deal with the Guilt of Sexual Failure for the
    Glory of Christ and His Global Cause," *Desiring God*, January 4, 2007,
    https://www.desiringgod.org/messages/how-to-deal-with-the-
    guilt-of-sexual-failure-for-the-glory-of-christ-and-his-global-
    cause.

24  Brené Brown, *Daring Greatly: How the Courage to Be Vulnerable
    Transforms the Way We Live, Love, Parent, and Lead* (New York: Avery,
    2012), 68.

25  Ephesians 2:8–9.

26  Laura Perry, *Transgender to Transformed: A Story of Transition That
    Will Truly Set You Free* (Bartlesville, OK: Genesis Publishing Group,
    2019).

27  Matthew 19:16–22.

28  Catie Edmondson and Annie Karni, "Have More Sex, Please!" *New
    York Times*, February 13, 2023, https://www.nytimes.com/2023/02/13/
    opinion/have-more-sex-please.html?smid=nytcore-ios-share&ref
    erringSource=articleShare.

29  Wiles, "15 Mind-Blowing Statistics."

30  Proven Men Ministries, "2014 Survey: Find Out How Many
    Christians Are Having Extramarital Sexual Affairs and How Porn
    Is the Igniting Fuel," *PR Newswire*, September 11, 2014, https://www.
    prnewswire.com/news-releases/2014-survey-find-out-how-many-c

hristians-are-having-extramarital-sexual-affairs-and-how-porn-i
s-the-igniting-fuel-274742051.html.

31 "U.S. Teen Girls Experiencing Increased Sadness and Violence,"
Centers for Disease Control and Prevention, February 13, 2023,
https://www.cdc.gov/nchhstp/newsroom/2023/increased-sadness-
and-violence-press-release.html.

32 1 Samuel 15.

33 2 Samuel 11.

# TELL ME YOUR STORY

We create safe places for others when we tell our stories. That's very powerful. So tell your story. Tell it all. Tell the good, the bad, and the ugly. Tell it to your friends. Tell it to those who look like they're hurting. Tell it until it doesn't feel so awkward anymore. Tell it until you can say it without stuttering. Tell it until it stops hurting to hear the agonizing details of it all. Tell it until it becomes part of your past that has shaped you and formed you into the compassionate person you are today. Tell it until God starts to use it to build bridges to those who are desperate and hurting and longing to find rest.

And in your healing, watch God heal others around you with His rest.

– From "Safe People"

**WWW.DRLINABOOK.COM**

# LIVING WITH POWER

## WE EQUIP CHRISTIANS TO LIVE WITH POWER BY...

- Sharing biblical truth for everyday life
- Sharing hope through humanitarian and medical aid to refugees

## LIVINGWITHPOWER.ORG

# ARE YOU DECONSTRUCTING?

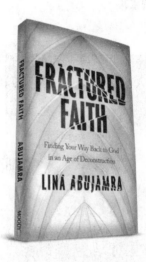

**What do you do when the faith you once held crumbles in the face of doubt, disillusionment, abuse, rejection, or injustice, even within the church?**

In Fractured Faith, Dr. Lina shares her own deeply personal experience with the near deconstruction of her faith – from the incredibly painful disillusionment of church hurt to the seeming absence of God in her pain. With her uniquely direct and diagnostic ER style, Dr. Lina leans into asking the hard questions about why people who once claimed to be Christians no longer believe.

Fractured Faith is a book about finding your way back to God...

Only to find out that He's been waiting for you all along.

# FOLLOW DR. LINA

| | |
|---|---|
| Instagram: | linaabujamra |
| Facebook: | facebook.com/lina.abujamra |
| | facebook.com/livingwithpower |
| TikTok: | linaabujamra |
| Twitter: | LinaAbujamra |
| Website: | livingwithpower.org |